THE SKIER'S BIBLE

1. *Junior Bounous, one of the finest American ski instructors.*

NEWLY REVISED EDITION

THE SKIER'S BIBLE

by Morten Lund

General Editor, *SKI MAGAZINE*

1972

Doubleday & Company, Inc., Garden City, New York

This book is dedicated to Bill Briggs,
ski teacher extraordinary,
and to my father, who put me on skis.

PHOTO CREDITS

Cover: World Champion Roger Staub at Vail, Colorado, where he is director of skiing. Photographed by Paul Ryan.

Ski Magazine: 1, 2, 3, 4, 52, 158, 253, 261, 263, 266, 281, 291, 294

Bohringer: 5

Frank Scofield: 19

John M. Stephens: 29, 297

Sun Valley News Bureau: 55, 58, 252, 262, 295

Stowe-News Bureau: 59, 62, 128, 281, 282

Prescott Fuller & Co., and Jay Peak, Inc.: 125

Ernie McCulloch: 264, 268

Tony Grauba: 265, 267

Hal Roberts: 269

Sun Valley Photo by Fred Lindholm: 270

Doner-Harrison, Inc.: 278

Bob McIntyre: 283

Sulo Oja: 284

Knut Edvard Holm: 285

Landesverkehrsamt in Salzburg: 286

Vermont Development Department: 288

Frederick, Big Bromley, Inc.: 289

Marvin Richmond: 290

Al Werthheimer: 292

C. J. Leabo: 293

Paul Ryan: 296

Scott Nelson: 293

OTHER BOOKS BY MORTEN LUND

The Expert Skier
The Snowmobiler's Bible

Library of Congress Catalog Card Number 77–164722
Copyright © 1968, 1972 by Morten Lund
All Rights Reserved
Printed in the United States of America
Revised Edition

Foreword

Morten Lund is easily one of the two or three top writers on ski technique in this country. His editorial collaboration with the leading ski school directors over the past fifteen years in writing basic and advanced theoretical articles has given him a breadth of experience that no other writer can match. In this book, he fills a long-standing need. Too often, ski books have been merely one exercise after another, without giving the skier a sense of where he is going and why. This book starts off by explaining with crystal-clear simplicity what each step of each system does for him in terms of his goals. The author takes the reader *inside* the world of teaching and tells the skier how to pick the best route for *his* individual needs.

This book ought to make both skier and ski instructor aware that there is more to ski learning than a set of standard steps. The author treats with insight the various classic and revolutionary methods at work on the American ski scene at present: his book includes the American and Canadian techniques, the Walter Foeger parallel school, Graduated Length Method with short skis. It includes methods used by several of the outstanding ski schools in the country. To my mind, there is no book like this one on the market today.

This book should make for better skiers and better ski instructors. It will certainly help its readers achieve an understanding of *all* teaching in the United States. This is something no other book has even attempted.

Taken altogether with the chapters on equipment, clothing, and safety, the presentation of technique and teaching methods makes this truly a *Skier's Bible*.

JUNIOR BOUNOUS

Provo, Utah
March 1972

Contents

FOREWORD 5

PREFACE 9

1. **MODERN SKIING** 11
   What modern skiing is and how it looks;
   how to learn it

2. **SPEED CONTROL** 23
   What the turn does for you; how one typical
   system builds the skier up to a parallel turn
   that controls his speed

3. **GRADUATED LENGTH METHOD:**
   SHORT TURNS ON SHORT SKIS 36
   How short skis let beginners make quick
   turns for maximum control on three-foot
   skis

4. **GRADUATED LENGTH METHOD:**
   LONGER SHORT SKIS 52
   How the skier "graduates" to longer skis;
   making longer turns at higher speeds on
   four- and five-foot skis

5. **WEDEL: SHORT TURNS ON LONG SKIS** 66
   How the Austrians started a revolution and
   how we use it today to control six- and
   seven-foot skis

6. **THE FOEGER SYSTEM** 76
   A system of parallel turning on six- and
   seven-foot skis from the beginning

7. **THE AMERICAN SYSTEM: STEM TURNS** 90
   The system of the great tradition; what stem
   turns can do for the skier by controlling speed on
   six- and seven-foot skis

8. **THE FIRST CHRISTIE TURNS OF
    THE AMERICAN SYSTEM**   99
    The early christie turns and how they lead
    toward full parallel turns

9. **ADVANCED AMERICAN TURNS**   108
    Parallel, wedel, and split rotation turns and
    how they are related

10. **SLOPE SAVVY**   124
    The problems of terrain and what the skier
    can do about them

11. **EASTERN AND WESTERN SKI TECHNIQUES**   133
    The inside story on ice—too little snow;
    the other extreme—too much snow

12. **EQUIPMENT I**   144
    What to do about spending money for gear

13. **EQUIPMENT II**   150
    Skis, poles, and clothes and how they relate to skiing

14. **SAFETY AND ETIQUETTE**   157
    Manners and minding your skiing make a better show

15. **COMPETITIVE SKIING, TOURING, AND
    ACROBATICS**   161
    Forms and impact of the alpine racer;
    the Nordic forms of the sport; flips and
    fancy skiing

16. **WHERE TO SKI**   169
    A rundown on the United States and Canada

Author's Preface

This book is, among other things, the first attempt within two covers to describe what all of the major ski-teaching systems in the country have to offer without trying to sell one system above all others. The book is—secondly—written specifically in the knowledge that the skiers of this country—eastern and western—are a different breed from skiers in Europe and the rest of the world.

The American skier plays on a higher level and plays at a faster pace. He skis better than any other country's recreational skiers. He tries harder. Although he's number one, he wants to get still better. He thinks in terms of skiing steeper trails and skiing them in all conditions. He believes technique to be the key to this magic realm of expert skiing.

The American instructor tries hard to oblige. He and his fellows have organized: their aim is to make skiing easier, to teach it faster.

The biggest and best-known instructors' group is the Professional Ski Instructors of America.

They teach "the American technique." There are also certified Canadian ski professionals. Third, there are the followers of the original Walter Foeger *Natur Teknik* school. Last, there are the Graduated Length Method teachers who apply the original insights of the Clif Taylor short-ski theory.

The primary aim of this book is to look into how the four major methods measure up to each other.

This book is also concerned with imparting the general know-how that the author has gleaned from twenty years of skiing and research. This includes his views on terrain, equipment, etiquette, safety, competitive skiing, and ski resorts in various parts of the United States and Canada.

Skiers who want to pursue the theory and practice of their sport in greater detail may wish to buy *The Expert Skier* by Morten Lund, scheduled for publication in 1973 by Doubleday & Company, Inc.

MORTEN LUND

Chapter 1

MODERN SKIING

What modern skiing is and how it looks; how to learn it

MODERN SKIING IS A MATTER OF PROPER BODY ACTION

The most valuable asset a skier can have in learning to ski, off the slope, is a book of good ski-sequence pictures to help him recognize good body action.

The choice of a good demonstrator for this book's ski-sequence photographs is thus very important; I was fortunate in obtaining the co-operation of Don Pearsons of the Killington, Vermont, ski school and Clif Taylor of Loveland, Colorado. Both are fine demonstrators of proper body action.

2. *Don Pearsons.*

3. *A parallel turn.*

4. *Hannes Schneider, founder of the Arlberg School of ski teaching, the first successful method in the history of the sport.*

*5. Touring in old-fashioned equip-
ment of the Hannes Schneider era.*

THE PLAN OF THE BOOK

The book begins with a look at the goals of skiing.

The best action to accomplish almost any turn is called "parallel." In parallel skiing, the skier keeps his skis pretty much pointed in the same (parallel) direction at all times.

Parallel skiing is a thing of beauty: the skier flows down the slope with a motion that is near to ballet. To master parallel is a joy in itself: the early chapters of this book deal with the look of the parallel turn and describe briefly a typical method of learning parallel. From there

we go to the wedel turn, that refinement of parallel technique that stands near the peak of achievement possible for most skiers.

Succeeding chapters show how various methods of teaching approach the goal of "long" parallel ski turns. Finally we turn to slope technique, clothes, equipment, and resorts.

A HISTORY OF SKI ACTIONS

The ski actions we see today have grown from a double root. One is the "stem" root, which began when Hannes Schneider of Austria

6. *The snowplow turn.*

7. *Running position.*

developed a method for teaching Austrian soldiers how to progress with skis in a "V" position, called a stem. The early Schneider school flourished in the Arlberg region of Austria. The Arlberg system thus still teaches the stem technique.

The other root, the parallel root, began with another Austrian, Toni Seelos. Herr Seelos was primarily a racer and a coach rather than an instructor. He never developed a strong method or system by which to teach his ski actions.

8. *Gravity, or "G," acts at "center of gravity" of ski and skier.*

9. *Each ski has its own G force, which acts to pull skis downhill.*

THE ARLBERG TECHNIQUE

Over many years, Schneider's school dominated the early ski-teaching business. Schneider came at a time when there were many conflicting kinds of ski action or "techniques" and he was able to clear them out in favor of the Arlberg kind of action. The Schneider school became so strong because it had the first true teaching method, a series of systematic steps which led to a technical goal.

The Arlberg technique was designed for utility. The stem turn could carry a soldier down a hill steadily and slowly. It allowed the civilian to ski in a loose "touring" binding, all that was available then. The solid, steady, and precise characteristics of the Arlberg turn fitted the times and the equipment.

A stem, quite simply, is a position with the ski tips together and the tails apart, so that the skier resembles a man riding a snowplow (Picture 6).

In fact, the stem and the "snowplow" are identical positions, but the terms designate different kinds of turns in the same position. (See Chapter 7.)

If we see a skier in a "running position" (Picture 7), that means he is going downhill. He will accelerate to higher and higher speeds unless something is done about it. One solution is a stem or a snowplow. Any skier can slow down considerably just by adapting this position.

Schneider proposed that the skier go into the stem whenever he felt he was going too fast. A proficient snowplow or stem skier can go down almost any mountain from top to bottom in a fairly straight line at slow speed, for the snowplow and stem act as brakes.

More than that, the snowplow or stem is a usable steering device.

How does the position actually *turn* a skier? The answer is simple, and also shows why some positions will *not* turn the skier.

S AND G FORCES

When a skier steps into place on a ski and stands normally, his center of gravity will be just to the rear of the center of the ski (Picture

10. *Resistance of snow, S_1 and S_2, pushes upward against skis.*

G and S pushing at different points tend to spin the skis toward each other

11. *S pushes up and G pulls down.*

12. *Series of snowplow turns leaves an S-shaped track down the hill.*

8) because bindings are always set a bit back on the ski. If we call the skier's weight "G," we can see that G is pressing down about where the skier's heel is fastened to the skis.

When a skier is in the snowplow, each ski has a force of gravity pulling it from that point. Essentially it means that we have G_1, the weight on one ski, and G_2, the weight on the other ski, both wanting to pull the skis straight down the hill (Picture 9). If there were no other forces involved, there would be no possibility of turning. The skier would have to go straight down the hill. If the skier were on a sheet of steel instead of snow, this would be the situation indeed.

But snow makes a difference. It provides a second force working on the skis. This is the *resistance* of the snow. This second force we can call S_1 and S_2. It pushes up the hill against the skis. It pushes at a point we can call the "center of resistance," which is just ahead of the middle of the ski, about where the toe of the skier's boot lies (Picture 10). In other words, while S pushes up at the skier's toe, G pulls down at the heel (Picture 11).

To reiterate:

G pulls downward just *behind* the center of the ski.

S pushes upward just *ahead* of the center of the ski.

If a log is pushed at two points in different directions, the log will swivel. Similarly, skis, pushed one way by G, and the other by S, will also turn. But each ski wants to turn differently. As you look at the picture, G_1 and S_1 are trying to spin one ski, at the left, in a counterclockwise direction, and G_2 and S_2 are trying to spin the other ski, at your right, in a clockwise direction. As long as both skis are trying equally hard to spin, it will be a standoff. The skier will not turn either way. He'll go straight down, with both skis trying to spin but not able to. All that will happen is that the skier will slow down.

But, if one ski could get a stronger spin than the other, this ski would win out and would spin in the direction it wanted and the skier with it. The skier would go down the slope in a slow spin. *This would constitute a turn* (Picture 13).

In order to turn, then, the skier merely puts more weight on one ski. Putting more weight on one ski increases that ski's tendency to spin. It wins out. Leaning on the right ski (Picture 13) causes the right ski to spin the skier counterclockwise. Leaning on the left ski (Picture 14) causes the left ski to turn the skier clockwise. The act of leaning is called "weight shift."

A skier can make one snowplow or stem turn after another simply by shifting his weight first to the one ski and then to the other. He will turn first to the left and then to the right, as in Picture 12. (See the skier's track.)

THE PARALLEL TURN

Turning in a stem or snowplow is fun but there is a more elegant way to turn, the way discovered by Tony Seelos not too long after Hannes Schneider had settled on his stem technique.

Take a skier in running position going down the hill (Picture 15). In "running position," his

13. *Snowplow turn to the left.*

14. *Snowplow turn to the right.*

15. *Running with skis parallel.*

16. *Turning with skis parallel.*

skis are pretty much together. Gravity (G) pulls him down the line of his skis. Snow resistance (S) opposes the skier head on. But if the skier can somehow pick up both skis a bit and skid them sideways at an angle to the original path

of the skis, (S) will come from the side. Both skis will go into a turn. The S and G forces are working to spin both skis in the *same* direction (Picture 16). This is much more powerful and efficient than a stem turn. In a stem,

skier jumps entire ski off

skier lifts tails off

the skis always fight each other, even though one wins out. In a parallel turn, both skis are together and the skis are helping each other out.

The parallel turn is made with S and G forces, like the stem turn, but the parallel turn is smooth and sophisticated: the skier balances over two skis together, rather than over two skis inelegantly far apart as in the stem-snow-plow position. The parallel turn is a graceful swoop compared to the dogged grind of the snowplow.

Because it looks good and because it works so well, parallel has been desirable ever since Seelos first mastered it as a racing technique; it has been the ideal of skiers for racing and recreation.

Almost all modern ski learning thus revolves around how to move the skis out of a straight path to *begin* the skid that starts a parallel turn. The way in which this is accomplished is part of "technique."

19. *The old-fashioned rotation method of turning. The skiers have "unweighted" and "blocked" the forward turn of arm and upper body. As a result, skis have skidded into the beginning of a parallel turn.*

Let's consider technique for a minute.

The skis need to be lifted a bit to get them out of the "groove" or "track" they have been running in. This "lift" can be provided by a short upward hop. Skiers call this hop "up-motion"; the result is "unweighting." (The skis go weightless for a second.) A quick hop can lift the whole ski off the snow (Picture 17).

A more sophisticated way to do it is to hop the tails off only, keeping the tips in contact with the snow (Picture 18).

Once the skier is in the air in this "un-weighted" position, he has to *turn* the skis. This calls for the exerting of some sort of muscle power *after* the hop. Gravity and the snow are not going to turn the skis for the skier while the skier is in the air. The skier himself must do it.

ROTATION PARALLEL TECHNIQUE

In the early days of technique, starting with Seelos, the "turning force" in the unweighted position was "rotation."

To use rotation to turn the skis, the skier has to wind up first while he is still on the snow.

That means he pulls his "outside arm" and shoulder back. ("Outside" refers to the outside of the turn.) Then, before he starts the hop, he swings this outside arm and shoulder forward by "rotating" his upper body from the waist up in the direction of the turn (Picture 19). Then he hops, and at the same time, stops or "blocks" this rotation motion. This blocking causes the turning movement of the upper body to carry the lower body around as well. The whole body therefore turns a bit, and the skis with it. The skier comes down again on the snow with the skis partly turned. From that point on, the S and G forces finish the turn for the skier, letting him swing around in a wide arc.

This is rotation.

Rotation is obviously a rather difficult, three-part kind of motion: windup, blocking, and turning. Not many skiers did it with ease. As a result, beginners did not learn parallel skiing very fast if at all. They tended to use stem skiing to start with and *never* skied parallel.

REVERSE PARALLEL TECHNIQUE

This was the situation in 1950 when a new phenomenon, a new kind of "turning power" began to replace rotation.

The new force was called "reverse."

Suppose you are standing on a small rug on a highly polished bare wood floor. If you want to turn your toes in an entirely new direction quickly, you would instinctively use "reverse turning power."

Try it. You will notice that in turning the feet around so that the toes point in another direction, the shoulder twists slightly in the direction *opposite* the foot turn (Picture 20). In other words, you will end up facing slightly farther left in order to make the toes point farther right.

The "reverse" action of the upper body provides a kind of leverage for the lower body so that it can turn quickly and forcefully.

The explanation of the effect is this: the muscles of the mid-body are the ones that twist

the lower body (and the feet with it) in a new direction. But these midsection muscles are fastened to the upper *and* lower body. To twist the lower body one way, they twist the upper body in the other, automatically.

Suppose a skier wants to make a reverse parallel turn. He goes down the slope (Picture 21); he hops up or unweights (Picture 22). Then, without any preliminary windup, he uses the mid-body muscles to twist the tips so that they turn in a new direction (more to the reader's left). The same muscles in the same move automatically turn the upper body in the opposite direction (to the reader's right, Picture 23). When he comes down, the skis will be turned; then the S and G forces will take over, and obligingly finish off the turn for him (Pictures 23 and 24).

What is so good about the "reverse"?

The reverse turn needs no preparatory windup. You can do it instantly. You can do

the newer "reverse" turning

20. *Reverse turning power on a small rug.*

many turns in rapid sequence, and this is impossible with the rotation turn. Much of modern skiing on slopes (and particularly slalom racing) demands faster and shorter turns for safety and control. It was inevitable that the reverse-powered turn should replace rotation, as it has to a great extent.

There are still times when it is convenient, more effective and fun, besides, to turn with rotation. Seelos' work was not all in vain. *The* modern turn, however, is the reverse turn.

THE QUESTION OF METHOD

The next big question is how to bring the beginning skier most quickly to the reverse parallel turn; the question is still in the process of being settled.

So, let's consider method, or the *way* in which we attain reverse parallel skiing.

Once you stem it's a real habit. The ideal system, obviously, would be to have the skier *start* on parallel turns, even rough parallel turns, so that he would never have to make a stem.

21

22

24. *Finish of a reverse turn.*

23. *A reverse parallel turn.*

The skier who could make parallel turns from the beginning would learn faster.

But, alas, the steps that compose the parallel turn are fairly sophisticated; there is the hop, the turning of the skis, the controlled sidewise and forward slice with the S and G forces finishing the turn for you. It requires good balance and a nice feel for the skis.

Ski teachers have persisted, therefore, in developing more sophisticated teaching methods.

Walter Foeger's *Natur Teknik* school confidently advertises that it can teach the average skier parallel from the first day on. A number of other schools use the *Graduated Length Method,* a way which makes it quite easy for skiers to do parallel turns from the beginning. Some American-system schools put students through the stem phases and onto the parallel much more quickly than before, through a "direct turning" philosophy.

Chapter   2

SPEED CONTROL

What the turn does for you; how one typical system builds the skier up to a parallel turn that controls his speed

When we consider the parallel turn, we must realize that in the beginning its most important function is to act as a brake, just as with the stem.

To understand this, consider a skier coming down the hill in running position. If he is coming straight down, he is running "in the fall line" (Picture 25) as we call it.

The fall line is an important idea in skiing:

it is a line that you always refer to in thinking about your turns. The fall line can be defined as the path a rolling object would take down the hill from a given point on the hill. For any given skier, the fall line runs straight down the hill from him.

Any path other than the fall line is called a "traverse."

A traverse, obviously, is a slower path down

25. *Skiing the fall line.*

26. *Skiing a traverse.*

27. *Slowing down by traversing.*

the hill than the fall line. But in the case of a steep traverse, as in Picture 26, it is not much slower.

Fortunately, there are also "shallow traverses," which are fairly slow paths (Picture 27).

One result of a parallel turn is to get the skier from the fall line or steep traverse into a shallow traverse. This traverse slows the skier down considerably. If he really wants to, he can even go from a shallow traverse to a horizontal traverse for a bit; then he'll soon stop (Picture 28). Obviously, then, a turn slows a skier down and even stops him by putting him on a shallow or horizontal traverse. But this is only the first way a turn slows the skier down.

The second slowdown factor is the drag effect of "slipping."

A ski that is turning cannot go straight ahead. To some extent, it has to skid sideways as it is moving. In the stem, for instance, the skier thrusts the tails of the skis out to the side with his legs so that the skis skid sideways. In the

28. *Stopping by traversing.*

29. *The skid effect of a turn is shown here. The skier throws snow to the outside of the turn, because the skis skid sideways as well as moving forward in the turn. Notice the flow of the snow out from under the tips to the outside, toward the reader.*

parallel, the skier uses his mid-body muscles to turn the skis into a sideways skid.

Sideways progress always takes place when a ski is turning. A ski can't turn without some slip (although in the case of the "carved turn" there is very little slip).

The spray of snow that the skis of a fast skier throws to the outside of a turn is a result of the braking effect (Picture 29) of slipping.

The turns that skiers make when they weave a snake trail down a slope are not made just for fun (although they are fun too); each little skid or slip has a *braking* effect, slowing the skier down and keeping him in control. The steeper the hill, the more turns are needed.

To recapitulate: a beginner confined to snow-plow turns would be going 40 miles an hour if he were on a steep slope: a snowplow takes some time to execute.

Parallel turns, on the other hand, can be executed much more quickly. The sooner the skier learns parallel, the sooner he is going to have control on the steep slopes. The progressive ski schools in the country are therefore bending every effort toward getting skiers to parallel quickly.

LEARNING PARALLEL

To get a rough idea of how many ski schools bring their skiers along to parallel, let's take a closer look at an advanced class being taught parallel by a typical method that has been called a "hop method." Most schools give the hop an important role. The skier, in one of his first exercises, stands in place and hops the tails of the skis to one side (Picture 30).

Note that the skier who hops the ski tails left, for instance, is doing approximately the same thing as a skier who swings the tips of his skis to the right. Both actions are right turns, in effect, and will serve to start the skis into the arc of a turn, the arc being finished off by S and G forces. As you can see by comparing Picture 31 with Picture 30, the skier who swings the tips left will have started just about the same kind of turn as a skier who hops the tails right. The hop takes a bit more energy because it moves the whole skier. The skier who swings his tips is merely twisting his feet in place.

Back to our class situation:

The skier first learns to hop the tails of the skis to one side, and simultaneously to turn the upper body to face that side. The skier stands with his ski tips at a certain point on a flat area (Picture 32), hops the tails to one side, faces that side, and lands with the tips still at point (1) (Picture 33).

This quarter turn of the upper body counterclockwise is really a reverse movement.

Or, to put it the way it is taught, "Hop tails left, face left." This is the reverse technique.

30. *Hopping the tails.*

31. *Twisting the tips.*

32. *Beginning the hop-and-reverse.*

original ski positions

new ski positions

33. *Finish of the hop-and-reverse.*

34. *Skis edged, not moving.*

35. *Skis flat, sideslipping.*

sideslip with turning

sideslip
without
turning

37

SIDE SLIDE

Now, after he had gotten the hop-and-reverse idea, the skier goes on to learn how to use snow and gravity to finish off the turn using S and G forces. This part of the teaching starts out with the slip or slide.

Any skier starting with skis pointed across the face of the hill can keep them there simply by "edging." He forces the upper edge of each ski into the snow by pressing his knees in toward the hill and, leaning out over the skis to maintain his balance, he puts most of the weight on the downhill or lower ski (Picture 34). He will *not* slide sideways downhill.

But if he now *flattens* the skis so that they lie against the slant of the hill, the skis will move sideways down the hill, slowly (Picture 35). This is sideslip or side slide.

In doing the side slide, the skier can stand so that his weight causes S and G to act at different points and turn the skis as the skier slides down (Picture 36). Or the skier moves his weight so that G acts at the same point as

S, then S and G neutralize each other and there is no turning of the skis (Picture 37). The skier has moved his weight a bit forward, and the skis slide down in a nice side slide *without* any turning of the skis.

UPHILL CHRISTIE

Next the skier does his first real turn, using the reverse motion to start it, and the S and G forces to finish the turn in a side slide with turning. This simple parallel turn is called the "uphill christie."

In the uphill christie, the skier runs along a traverse (Picture 38). When he flattens his skis and makes a reverse motion, the tails of the skis move downhill and the skis start sliding sideways and turning (Picture 39). Then the G forces working from the side keep the skis turning (Picture 40).

The skier is now moving forward, his skis are slipping, and the tips are turning away from the valley, up the hill. (This is why it is

38. *Running.*

straight
original
path

tails
move
downhill

new
curving
path

39. *Starting the turn without hop.*

40. *S and G forces continue the turn.*

called the *uphill* christie.) When the skis turn far enough, the skier will be running in a shallow traverse and will be slowed down (Picture 40).

This turn is not quite so simple as it seems, however. The flattening of the skis is a fairly subtle process. The beginning skier is not used to exerting this fine a control. That is, he is not used to holding the raised edges of the skis precisely an inch less or an inch more toward or away from the snow. Making a ski lie "flatter" or "more on edge" is hard to accomplish until the skier has practiced it many times.

Therefore, in a typical method, the skier uses

the hop that he learned at a standstill (Pictures 32 and 33) to start the ski turning. The skier first goes into a crouch (Picture 41). Then he hops (Picture 42). Then he uses the reverse motion to turn the skis (Picture 43). The minute the tails are turned off the track by the skier's reverse motion, of course, some skidding takes place, and the S and G forces go to work turning the ski.

This "crouch, hop, and reverse" is a way of forcing the uphill christie to happen. And it does happen, even if the skier's edge control is a bit ragged.

41. *Running.*

42. *Starting the turn with a hop.*

43. *S and G forces continue the turn.*

CHRISTIE FROM THE FALL LINE

The skier who has reached the point where he can make the turn up the hill from a shallow traverse is now on the way to making a parallel turn of a more demanding sort.

He first makes his uphill christie from a somewhat steeper traverse, and then from a still steeper traverse (all on a moderate slope). Finally, he makes the turn from the fall line.

This means that, having started a run down the fall line and having gone for a distance, he crouches and hops and makes his reverse. There follows a long turning slide as the S and G forces take over to finish the turn (Picture 44).

This turn is called a "christie from the fall line."

Also, it can be described as "the last half of a full parallel turn."

THE FULL PARALLEL TURN

The full parallel turn starts with the tips turning "down the hill," and ends with tips turning up the hill. Thus, the parallel turn can be thought of as having these two parts (Picture 45): the first part, in which the skier turns the tips from the shallow traverse down the hill into the fall line (Positions A through C), and the second, where the skier turns the tips out of the fall line up the hill back to the new traverse (Positions C to E).

This latter part is nothing but a "christie from the fall line."

The second part of the parallel is easiest. Here, the skier is continuously slowing down as he comes out of the fall line, because he is headed for a shallow traverse. In the first part of the turn, going steeper and steeper into the fall line, he is speeding up. Obviously, when the skier starts trying the first part of the turn, he'd better know the second part by heart, so that he can pull out of the turn easily and quickly and come to a gradual slowdown.

44. *Christie from the fall line.*

THE USES OF MOMENTUM

In the first part of the full parallel turn, we can say that the G force includes the "momentum," that force due to the skier's forward speed.

The force built up by the skier's speed along a path will tend to make him continue that path. When the skis are twisted or hopped out of that path (with or without the help of a ski pole) and started out in a new direction, momentum and the G force both then will push the tails of the skis toward the outside of the turn. The S force comes along to push the tips toward the center of the turn (Pictures 46 and 47).

A first traverse

B

fall line

C

skis
turn
downhill

D

E

new traverse

45. *Full parallel christie.*

46. *G force in a traverse.*

47. *G force in the parallel turn down the hill.*

48. *Middle of a full parallel turn.*

49. *End of a full parallel turn.*

The skier can finish off the parallel turn simply by holding his position: this is a question of balancing over the outside ski and letting the S and G forces do the rest of the work (Pictures 48 and 49).

This full parallel turn is the goal of all first-year skiers.

POLE HANDLING

Since we have mentioned poles for the first time, it should be said that, in the modern theory of recreational skiing, you should be able to do all turns on moderate terrain without the use of poles. Poles are really necessary on steep terrain only.

The function of the pole is to help the skier hop or rise in the unweighting movement. The pole should be placed in the snow pointing pretty much in the same direction as the skis. If you plant the pole so that the tip points in toward the skis, then the chances are that you are trying to "hook" yourself into the turn with the pole, instead of using reverse or rotation to start the turn.

Most beginners tend to put their hand through the loop of the pole strap and then grasp only the pole. This is wrong. Pictures 50 and 51 show that the hand is put through the loop and then *both* the loop and the pole are grasped. This positions your hand properly on the pole handle. When using the pole, let the strap take the strain. You don't need to clench the pole hard. In fact, if you use the strap properly, you can leave your hand partly open and relaxed as you use the pole (Picture 51).

THE GOAL OF ALL METHODS

The ultimate goal of all systems is the same: the full parallel turn, starting in one traverse and finishing in the traverse going in the opposite direction. There is no fundamental disagreement among schools.

What we have, rather, is an exact illustration

50. *Putting the hand through the pole loop.*

51. *Grasping the pole and the loop.*

of the difference between "method" and "technique."

Obviously, a reverse-turn skier would *look* different to a marked degree from a rotation skier on the slope; here we would say that these *techniques* are different.

Yet, two fully trained reverse system skiers would look pretty much the *same,* given minor latitude in arm positions and other details regardless of the fact that they were taught by different schools. Thus, here in the case of the two reverse skiers who look the same, the *technique* is the same, but the *method* of reaching it was different.

The purpose of this chapter has been to give you an idea of how a typical ski-teaching system puts together a ladder of progress, a method of learning a turn that controls speed.

In the succeeding chapters, we shall take up the various methods taught by the distinct schools operating on the American continent.

A word about method.

While method is important, particularly if you are going to teach yourself (a goal of this book is to help you teach yourself), there is no substitute for a good teacher. The ski instructor who teaches well by an old-fashioned method is preferable to a poor instructor teaching a new method.

The skier who reads this book should not be quick to blame a system. The best advice is "find a teacher you like" and stick with him. If you have a good teacher, it is worth paying him for a private lesson; you will learn faster.

Let's review a few terms we have run across in the previous pages.

turn—any curved path made by the skis.

fall line—the steepest way down the hill from any given point on the hill.

traverse—any straight path other than the fall line.

christie—a sliding turn, or the sliding part of any turn. (The name comes from Christiania, the old name of Oslo, capital of Norway; the turn was invented in the neighborhood.)

uphill christie—a turn from a steep traverse to a shallower traverse with skis parallel. The easiest parallel turn.

turn uphill—same as uphill christie.

turn out of the fall line—same as uphill christie, but starting in the fall line instead of in a traverse.

edge control—the ability to flatten the skis or put them on edge as required by circumstances.

method—the way in which technique is acquired.

technique—the final "look" of the skier derived mainly from the kinds of turning power that he employs.

turn into the fall line—a turn that goes from a traverse into the fall line.

turn downhill—same as turn into the fall line.

full turn—a turn from a traverse into the fall line and then out of the fall line again, to a traverse in the opposite direction: a turn downhill followed by a turn uphill.

sideslipping—going sideways downhill by flattening the skis against the hill until they start sliding sideways, without turning.

side-sliding—same as sideslipping.

Chapter 3

GRADUATED LENGTH METHOD: SHORT TURNS ON SHORT SKIS

How short skis let beginners make quick turns for maximum control on three-foot skis

This chapter will take up the idea of making many short turns to get the *maximum* in speed control.

Even with parallel turns, there is difficulty in making them short enough to get really good control. When you watch a well-trained skier come down an expert slope, you see him bobbing in a continuous up-and-down rhythm, rising and crouching for each turn. He keeps the skis' speed down by these turns and it is a beautiful piece of work to watch.

If only beginners could get something approximating this kind of control, they would be better off right from the start. Short turns equal safety.

But the co-ordination needed to harmonize the hops and the reverse motions with the pole work for short turns is obviously quite beyond the skill of even the best of beginners.

The only way would be to make the skis "easier," somehow.

The solution came through Clif Taylor, previously an instructor in the ski school at Hogback Mountain, in Brattleboro, Vermont. Taylor had some pupils who were experimenting on their own in the use of shorter skis. They simply sawed off the tails of old pairs of long skis. Taylor became intrigued, because it seemed to help their skiing, and he designed a pair of

52. *Clif Taylor, inventor of the short ski, does a quick jump in his shortest version, the three-foot ski.*

five-foot skis (normal skis run six feet or longer) for his pupils. They worked better than sawed-off skis. Taylor's pupils were happy, and they skied better than ever.

Taylor now began to think about ski lengths in earnest. He wondered how short you could make a ski and still have something skiable. He

counter-
clockwise
motion of
upper
body
and
arms

clockwise
motion of
lower body
and skis

53. *Turning while standing on one spot.*

experimented with four-foot designs and then with even shorter ones. He got down to a three-foot design, which would just hold a boot and a binding. He obtained good results with the four-footers and the three-footers in his beginning classes. Almost anyone could start skiing on the three-footers without much strain.

THE TWIST METHOD

After a bit of experimenting, Taylor also found that by using a "twist" turning process he could get people to make short, connected parallel turns the *first* day they got on skis. The beauty of it, Taylor found, was that the three-footers needed no "hop" to start them turning. They could be *twisted* into the turn with a reverse motion only. Taylor had thus essentially reduced the complexity of turning parallel by reducing the size of the skis. The "twist" teach-

ing technique, added to short skis, brought about a revolution.

The first step of the Taylor *method* is to have the skier swing the skis while standing in place on the flat. The lower body swings with the skis, and the upper body swings in the opposite direction, so that we get a series of quick, reverse-powered turns in place (Picture 53).

This same twist is next done while the skier moves down the hill (Picture 54). The turn is short so there is very little time for the S and G forces to act. The Taylor method therefore makes the kickoff of the turn, the reverse-power movement, all-important. This simplifies things tremendously. The Taylor twist (Picture 53) is related to the "hop and twist" of the previous chapter, but Taylor's exercise is much easier and less acrobatic.

What can the beginning skier get out of the Taylor system?

In the first place, he can go up the ski lift within a few hours of getting on the skis. By

traversing

turning

54. *Turning while moving down the hill.*

55. *The old-fashioned hanging-in-the-straps kind of turn, no longer taught today.*

contrast, the American-system skiers and the Foeger-system skiers will have to wait more than a day, at minimum, and more likely as much as two days, before they get their long skis sufficiently under control to go up a ski lift. The users of the short ski have more fun.

The skier on short skis gets tremendous *motivation.* He can make a *series* of parallel turns. He is *able* to make turns right away, and these are the parallel turns he wants to perfect. He doesn't have to detour into different *kinds* of turns along the way.

One of the hardest things for beginners to do is to connect their turns, one after the other. And yet, closely connected turns mean safety and control. The rhythm that can be worked up on the short skis is exactly the same reverse-powered rhythm (with the hopping or bobbing motion left out) that must be achieved on long skis if one is to do well on steeper slopes.

Third advantage: he is making *short* turns.

He is not likely to learn short turns to begin with by any other method in most ski schools. Other ski schools—American, Foeger, and Canadian—have to urge the *long* parallel turn upon the pupil before he has mastered a *short* parallel turn. The short parallel gives the skier the best control, since it is quicker than the long parallel.

Fourth advantage: the skier can progress by stages, using short, controlled turns all the time —three-foot ski, four-foot ski, five-foot ski, up to as long as the skier can handle. By these very gradual stages he can achieve expertise easily. This is called today the Graduated Length Method, or "GLM," and is taught by at least twenty-five leading schools today, coast to coast.

Graduated Length Method is now part of the Head Ski Company's "Head-Way" system, which is being installed at ski areas on a franchise basis by Karl Pfeiffer, formerly head of the ski school at Killington, Vermont, and now with Head Ski Company.

The use of the short ski raises a question.

HOW LONG SHOULD A SKI BE?

The traditional answer to proper ski length, the one that most skiers and ski-shop salesmen will give you, is that the proper length of ski for the beginning skier runs from the heel of the skier's upraised palm down to the floor, when the skier is holding his hand straight up overhead.

This is, as any racer will tell you, the proper length for a racing ski. Most shops are thus selling beginners a racing-length ski, which is about as sensible as selling an "Indianapolis 500" racing car to a housewife.

Fortunately, the palm-to-floor-length rule is slowly giving way, mostly under the impact of the short-ski idea. Many instructors have told me that, as a rule of thumb, they prefer to see the *average* skier with skis a foot shorter than racing length. And they like to see a *beginner* start with three-foot skis and during the first year buy skis no taller than himself.

The real test of the proper length is not a rule of thumb, but the longest ski you can handle on the slopes you want to ski with the ability you now have.

Taylor's phrase for it is "I'd rather have the challenge in the mountain than in the skis."

Why go on to long skis at all if the short skis are so easy?

The first answer is pride in having skis as long as everybody else's. There is nothing wrong with legitimate pride.

A more practical reason is this: the longer ski is like a longer wheel base in a car. It gives a smoother ride. The long ski goes over bumps more easily, it goes through abrupt potholes in better fashion, and it is generally easier-riding at high speeds.

Another practical reason is that the long ski has more speed. You may not want more speed down a steep slope, but it is nice to have speed on the long, flat runouts at the bottom of the mountain.

A third practicality concerns soft snow. The shorter skis tend to sink or nose in unless the skier sits way back on the skis. The long ski will not need so much change of balance except in deep powder, in which case you have to sit back on the long ski as well.

The advantages of the long ski can be seen as incentives for the skier to improve so that he can handle longer skis, rather than as incentives to get longer skis than he can handle.

SCHOOLS THAT TEACH GLM

There is another practical problem: there are quite a few ski schools that do not take pupils on three- or four-foot skis. I think that these schools are mistaken in their attitude; however, there are plenty of schools that do teach GLM today. There is a list of some of the most outstanding ones at the end of Chapter 4.

PROPER STANCE FOR SHORT SKIS

It used to be that the skier leaned way out ahead of his boots, "hanging in the straps" (Picture 55). But this is now a thing of the past. The modern skier leans forward but not very far.

56. Modern long-ski position.

57. Modern short-ski position.

The beginning skier on short skis is encouraged to "stand over his binding," that is, to lean neither forward nor back, weight squarely over the boots in a loose, relaxed stance.

Short skis have been criticized for lacking the stability of the longer skis. You can't lean forward to "drive the skis." This is true, but not relevant. The proper stance for the beginner is over the boots, not leaning forward or back.

The skier who finds that short skis are unstable usually is standing with the weight too far forward or too far back as he skis. This is something he might get away with if he started on long skis. On short skis he must ski over the boots.

FIRST SHORT-SKI TURNS

We'll continue our discussion of the short-ski method. The Taylor method is a simple one to understand.

The individual major steps in the Taylor system are all full turns, right from the beginning, unlike the first steps in long-ski systems. The first turns in the Taylor system will tend to be executed roughly by the learning skier, but that doesn't mean that the end result won't be satisfactory. The skier sees that he can *make* the skis turn at every step along the way; his motivation remains strong throughout the course.

The mid-muscles of the body supply the power for the entire turn, almost. This "active" turning power constitutes what I call "direct turning," as opposed to the classic "carved" turns, in which the skier relies a great deal on the passive S and G forces to finish the turn. This is "passive turning."

Direct turning is much simpler than passive turning; the latter involves the delicate business of getting just the right amount of edge on a ski so that it will move nicely into a long passive turn.

The Taylor system starts out on three-foot

58. *Graduated Length Method skis.*

59. *Turning counterclockwise on a rug.*

skis, goes on to four-foot skis, then five-foot skis, and finally to the skier's own six- or seven-foot skis (Picture 58).

The turn on three-foot skis can be practiced indoors (Picture 59). The skier takes a small rug and stands on a smooth floor; he can even do it in stockinged feet. He stands with arms out to the sides and twists his feet back and forth in rapid succession.

The "back and forth in rapid succession" signals that the reverse motion has to be used. This continuous twisting can only be done by reverse power. The twisting, once started, is carried on for a considerable time. The skier must get rhythm, as in a dancing lesson. At each beat he makes a twist "left-right." And then "right-left." It goes "left-right, right-left, left-right," and so on.

THE EXTENDED ARMS

An important factor is holding the arms to the sides. Let's look at this for a minute.

The mid-muscles of the body in the "twist," or reverse motion, are forcing the feet and the upper body to turn opposite each other. The feet *must* turn in one direction (assuming there's not too much friction under them) when the upper body turns explosively in the opposite direction.

If the skier could grab a handy door frame with both hands, he could twist the feet *without* moving the upper body in space. He would be able to twist the feet much harder, too, since *all* the muscle force could be directed to the feet and none would be used to turn the upper body.

Extending the arms to the sides is in effect something like grabbing a door frame. The outstretched arms increase the resistance of the upper body to being turned (not quite as much as a door frame would, of course). With the arms increasing the resistance of the upper body to turning, more of the muscle force goes to turning the feet and the skis. In other words, with the arms out, the skis will turn that much more easily.

60. *Turning feet clockwise indoors.*

61. *Turning skis clockwise outdoors.*

62. *Turning skis on "up" bounce.*

63. *Finishing turn as bounce ends.*

Of course, you have to do your bit to keep the skis friction-free. Keep them good and flat on the snow and bounce a little, gently, up and down, as you twist.

One important thing to notice about the rug exercise is the *mental* emphasis on twisting the feet. Concentration on turning the feet makes the feet turn more powerfully. There is nothing magic about this. It is simply that, in order to turn the feet effectively, the twist motion has to be started "explosively." Concentrating on moving the feet is a way of starting the movement "explosively."

When the skier can make ten or twenty turns back and forth without interruption, he is ready to go outdoors.

By comparing Pictures 60 and 61, the reader can see that the movement is just the same, indoors or out.

The skier gets on a pair of three-foot skis and picks a well-packed spot on the flat. It should be good and hard. In fact, "boiler-plate" snow is about the best thing to have for the first Taylor exercise outdoors.

TWISTING IN PLACE

Once the skier is in place with his three-footers, he starts his twist motion. He moves the ski tips: left-right-left. The resistance of snow is much greater, naturally, than that of a slippery floor. The twist motion on snow has to be definitely *much more explosive* in order to achieve any turning of the skis at all. The skier *must* hold his arms out to the sides horizontally (Pictures 62 and 63).

Two more things will help the skier to move the skis back and forth evenly. The first is pressing the knees and boots together. This provides a solid support for the skier and allows him to turn the skis together, rather than one after the other.

The second is a *slight* bounce. (Not a hop off the snow. Complete "unweighting" is not needed here.) A slight, regular bounce aids the

rhythm of the skier and reduces friction under the ski. The bounce should be timed so that the skier is *up* when the skis start moving through the arc. He comes down for a fraction of a second as the skis stop at the end of each arc. It is an "up and twist" (Picture 62) and "down and stop" (Picture 63). Notice in Picture 63 that Taylor has a slight knee bend. He has come down from his bounce and is ready to bounce again.

If the snow is soft, the skis will dig themselves down after a number of arcs. This makes it harder to turn. The skier, therefore, should move to a new, smoother spot.

If the weight is too far forward, the skis will turn hard, and the same if the weight is too far back. The skier should move his weight back and forth over his skis until he finds the spot over the skis where the skis turn most easily.

If the weight is centered over the middle of the running surface of the ski, as it should be, the ski will make a neat hourglass pattern in the snow. The tips and tails of the skis each make their own separate little arcs in the snow, while the middle of the skis stay pretty much in place. This is what makes the hourglass pattern (Pictures 64 and 65). The top and bottom of the hourglass pattern will be about the same size if the weight is centered. If the arc at the tip of the skis is largest, the weight is too far back, and if the arc at the tail of the skis is largest, the weight is too far forward.

EFFECT OF BINDING POSITION

If the skier mounts bindings on his own skis, or even if a shop mounts them, he has to watch for the position of the boot on the ski. The ball of the foot (widest part of the boot) should be over the *center* of the running surface of the ski. The running surface is the flat part of the ski in contact with the snow. If the boots are mounted too far back on short skis (common in many cases), the skier will have to lean too far forward to get his weight centered. If they are

64. *Hourglass pattern: front view.*

65. *Hourglass pattern: side view.*

mounted too far forward, the skier will have to sit back too far.

OUTDOOR PRACTICE

There are two good exercises for outdoor short-ski practice. The first is to have another skier grasp the hands of the skier who is trying to twist in place. This gives the solid support necessary to get the skier started in the rhythm (Picture 66).

The second, which is another way of increasing the skier's leverage, is simply to stick two poles into the snow. The skier uses them in the same way he might use another skier's hands, to help him get started with the twist. However, if either or both bridging sequences are used, the skier should get back to the main exercise of twisting in place, using only his outstretched arms to help him stabilize the upper body.

Poles are normally *not* used in the short-ski technique until the skier is on the longest skis that he is going to be using for a while. The reason for this is that the poles interfere with learning the twist down the hill. It is too easy for the skier to stick poles into the snow while he is going down the slope. He is trying to brake himself with the poles instead of relying on the braking effect of the turns. Poles can completely disrupt the necessary rhythm of the Taylor system.

The skier should do the twist in place until he can make ten turns back and forth without stopping. The idea is to build up the feel for rhythm and balance on the short skis before taking them down the slope (Picture 67). In the Taylor method, this is where the skier gets his "reverse-motion reflex" built up. Thirty minutes of twisting in place on the snow is probably enough for most skiers; less might be too little. The twisting should be continued until it is almost automatic, like the steps of a dance. The dance simile is not far wrong if we think of the beautiful co-ordination of a wedel skier on the slopes on long skis.

66. *Holding pupil (left) to help start twist.*

67. *Two beginners twisting in place.*

TWISTING DOWN THE SLOPE

The next thing the skier does is practice the twist while he is going down the slope (Pictures 68 and 69). The skier has to take into account his speed down the hill, but with three-footers the speed is not very great. Usually the first turns come easily (Picture 70). To balance and twist properly, the skier must keep his arms out to the sides, a subtle but necessary position. The arms should be held out in a loose, relaxed manner, the wider the better (Picture 71), but not stretched out to the last inch.

The skier must keep his skis *flat* on the snow during the twist. Preferably, he should squeeze

68. *Running down fall line.*

69. *Twisting into a turn.*

70. Turning from a traverse.

71. Wide stance.

his skis and his knees together, although if it is more comfortable for him to take a wider stance and separate the skis a bit for stability, that is all right too (Picture 71). The skier need not emphasize form at this point. It is more important that he twist the skis in a series of turns.

The action of gravity, added to the simple twisting motion, will produce turns once the skier actually makes these twists as he moves (Picture 72).

The skier starts his twist explosively. Otherwise, he will just be "steering" the small skis back and forth across the hill in long turns. This kind of steering doesn't lead to parallel skiing. Long steered turns on short skis waste the potential of the short ski for teaching short parallel turns. The turns should be short, explosive, and with a flat ski.

A problem will show up at this stage—"catching the outside edge." When the skier is making a turn with fairly flat skis, the edge of the ski on the outside of the turn runs the danger of catching in the snow, and the skier trips himself. The skier *will* catch some outside edges to begin

with, in the very nature of things. Falls on three-footers are not serious (Picture 73), and the skier will soon learn to keep the outside edge of the ski up just a bit. This is usually instinctive. If his falls keep recurring, the skier may have to keep the skis apart at first.

72. Series of twists leaves snakelike track.

73. *Falling is not a problem.*

The terrain for the first short-ski exercise should be gentle, of course, with a flat runout at the bottom so that the skier will come to a stop by himself if he doesn't succeed in making good turns on the very first run. The snow should be fairly hard, and it is absolutely necessary to pack it down, if it is soft.

This is a crucial condition for success. Once the skier can make turns on a packed slope, he can make them in soft snow. Once he builds his confidence in his ability to make the skis turn, he can do it almost anywhere under any conditions, but the first turns have to be successful to give him confidence.

A packed slope will also reduce the number of caught edges considerably. (So will holding the skis a bit apart.)

The skier should not try to make too many corrections in his skiing at this stage. One practical advantage of the short skis is that so many factors can be *ignored*. The skier can put his entire attention on making the turns. He goes on. He gets his corrections later, when he has a bit more experience and when, above all, he *knows* he is going to be able to ski, so that corrections don't seem to be a life-or-death matter. The three-foot-ski learner doesn't even need to keep his skis together at first if he feels most stable

skiing with them apart. He can turn the skis simultaneously just as easily if they are six inches apart as when they are edge to edge once he gets the hang of the turning. A distance between the skis is also a help in keeping the outside edges clear.

However, one fault to avoid early is "arm-waving."

Many skiers attempt to "steer" the skis with the arms. This amounts to a "rotation" type of turn. The arms should stay out at the sides. They should be moved opposite to the direction of the tips. The turn should start in the movement of the *lower* body, which kicks the skis into the turn.

Apart from these considerations, the skier does not have to get into much detail about body position or anything else. If he can make *short* turns, he should be satisfied. Stopping to correct faults when the turns are going well is *wrong*. It throws away the most precious advantage of short-ski learning: the chance to build up reverse reflex and balance and feel for the skis while *underway*. The skier who stands around in class watching others is wasting his time at this stage. He should be out experiencing his reactions to the skis, logging some mileage and stopping to correct only if he is not able to continue making short turns.

SHORT TURNS

The turns should not be long carved turns (Picture 74). This is fine for experienced skiers, but the beginning skier needs to stick with the idea of connecting short turns (Picture 75). The turns *must* be short, and to do this, the skis must be kept flat, so that they slew around. If the skier finds that he cannot do this readily, he needs some practice sideslipping. He may have to learn to flatten the ski to make slipped or slewed turns. His instructor or a better skier should ski with him to help him start turning (Picture 76).

The first day on short skis should see the skier concentrating on skiing down the hill. If he can

74. *A long looping turn.*

76. *Instructor skiing with student.*

75. *Short tight turns.*

get a few miles under his belt, all other things will come much more easily. On this day, his whole attitude toward the sport is being formed. If the first day's work is worrisome and painful, the skier's mental set toward skiing will be negative and it will take him a lot to regain a positive attitude. If, on the other hand, he has a wonderful time, he will be able to endure a lot of detailed correcting later on without getting impatient with himself or his teacher. He *knows* skiing is fun.

This concept of learning, incidentally, is a basic psychological concept that extends even

77. *Running in a traverse.*

78. *Turning uphill from a traverse.*

to animals: the learning processes should be connected with pleasure, if the learning is to proceed well. In training a seeing eye dog, for instance, the trainer makes sure that the young puppy has plenty of play and very little training. If a seeing eye dog is taken into strict training during puppyhood, he becomes a balky, unmanageable adult dog.

Another thing to remember is that the whole process of learning to ski is to a certain extent outside the voluntary control of the skier. No matter how much of a "natural" he is, it takes a given amount of time for his motor reflexes to build up and for his mind to develop satisfactory sensitivity to the right "feel," particularly in regard to balance and edging. The more fun a skier has, the faster the reflexes build up, because a skier who is having fun is a skier willing to go up and down the slopes all day long and take his small mishaps in stride. The active, moving skier gets the needed experience much faster than his cousin who stands and watches others. This is true even though the cousin may be inherently better co-ordinated.

The only serious drill that the short-ski pupil needs, outside the twist motion, is to learn to hold the turn so that he is heading across the hill and can easily come to a stop. This is something he should feel able to do (Pictures 77 and 78). Turning to a horizontal traverse and stopping gives the skier a chance to rest.

Before he goes up the lift, the skier should spend a bit of time climbing up and twisting while going down. Climbing is very good exercise and develops a feel for the skis.

Climbing on short skis is not a problem. The skier can side-step the skis up the hill simply by putting enough edge on the skis and putting them down firmly, sideways into the slope; the skis will bite in and hold (Picture 79).

Or, he can herringbone up the hill. To do this, he faces uphill and walks up in a knock-kneed position, putting the weight on the inside edge of the skis so they bite into the hill (Pictures 80 and 81).

The same climbing steps are used for long skis as well.

79. *Side-stepping uphill.*

80. *Herringbone uphill: rear view.*

81. *Herringbone uphill: front view.*

Short skis often work out very well for small skiers. They find it easier to climb up and ski down with three-foot skis than with the longer ones. Long skis mean using the snowplow, which is not so easy for the younger set (Picture 82).

The beginning skier on three-foot skis often can go up the lift at a ski area within an *hour* of

82. *Short kids on skis too long.*

83. *Short kids on short skis.*

first getting on the skis. This is not true of the skier who starts on long skis; rather it should not be true. (Self-taught beginners sometimes get on a lift line before they even begin to get used to their long skis, with very bad results.)

For the short-ski learner, the lift makes it possible to cover a great deal of territory. His first day will be glorious.

Chapter 4

GRADUATED LENGTH METHOD: LONGER SHORT SKIS

How the skier "graduates" to longer skis; making longer turns at higher speeds on four- and five-foot skis

In this chapter the Taylor system connects with other systems, including the American, Foeger and Canadian as the Taylor skier goes to four- five- and six-foot skis. It's made for today's learners.

Today, people who want to learn to ski are not as "serious" as they were five or ten years before. They want to learn, but they also want to enjoy it *soon*. They have been promised they *will* enjoy it by countless magazine, radio, and TV pronouncements. They may quit the sport if they are disappointed.

Hannes Schneider's sequence was primitive. The skier was first put into the snowplow position and drilled until, by dint of repetition, he could do the snowplow. Then he was put into the stem turn and drilled in that. There were enough well-to-do skiers who had the time and money to undergo the drill to fill up a few ski schools in Austria. But when this system was first tried upon tens of thousands of ordinary people in the United States, a country where the average skier did not have the time or money to undergo the almost military indoctrination of the Arlberg system, the dropout rate was spectacular.

The United States ski schools, therefore, have been strongly motivated to find faster ways of getting progress. Some have adopted GLM (see the list at the end of this chapter). Others have refined their long-ski sequences considerably. Junior Bounous, director at Snowbird, Utah, has produced teaching sequences that he has constantly worked over, sequences that have been published to some extent by *Ski Magazine* and that have evoked widespread admiration. "Good sequences are the reason for a ski school's repeat business," said Bounous. (In his work Bounous was helped in developing and organizing the sequences by Bill Briggs, a particular friend of mine and the canny ski school director of the ski school at Storm King, Jackson, Wyoming.)

SHORT-SKI SEQUENCES

After a skier has conquered the initial twist turns and can go on, he begins the Taylor sequences in preparation for skiing on fourfooters; he gets ready to "graduate" to his second step in the Graduated Length Method.

In the first preparation exercise, the skier on three-foot skis puts a glove between his knees

84. *Junior Bounous, who has headed ski schools in California and Utah. His "sequences" have been widely copied in the country's ski schools.*

and twists down the hill squeezing the glove. This makes the skier keep the knees close together, and the skis consequently will be closer too: this helps with longer skis.

The next exercise teaches the skier to twist his skis by using different portions of the body. First, he goes down the slope twisting the skis with a twist at the ankle. This makes a series of "ankle turns" of very small arc (Picture 85). Then he goes down twisting the entire legs from thigh on down. This makes a series of slightly larger "leg turns." Finally, he goes down the slope twisting the whole lower body from the waist down, making bigger "hip turns" (Picture 86). In the subsequent lessons, as the skis get bigger, the skier finds he has to make use of the longer, bigger turns to get the skis moving in rhythm.

The next bridging exercise to four-footers: the skier picks up one ski and twists down the hill on the other. This improves the balance, and the skier will become conscious of the fact that the weight can go on either ski.

The last bridging exercise is bouncing. The bounce, which the skier may or may not have used in his early twisting on three-footers, is necessary with the four-footers. The skier should practice bouncing as he goes down the slope on three-footers, with an "up" as he starts to twist and a "down" as he ends the twist. It will make for smoother skiing on the threes and build up the rhythm on the fours.

Bouncing does *not* mean that the skier hops the skis in the air. Hopping is hard to do on short skis; trying to do so will hold the skier back. (One purpose of the short ski is to elim-

85. *Foot turns.*

86. *Lower body turns.*

87. *Twising clockwise on four-footers on one spot.*

inate the need for the hop. To hop adds an unnecessary difficulty and lengthens the whole process of learning on short skis.)

The three-foot stage should not have taken more than two days. A good skier can manage with one day. At the end of that day he will be able to get down a beginning intermediate slope. He then goes onto four-foot skis.

A certain proportion of skiers, perhaps one out of eight, will not be able to go on four-footers immediately. They will need more work on the three-footers. They can stay with their class on the three-footers, which is much more satisfactory than being left behind.

TWISTING ON FOUR-FOOTERS

The skier on four-foot skis starts off in much the same way as he did on three-foot skis. The

88. *Twisting counterclockwise on four-footers on one spot.*

89 to 90.
Twisting down the slope on four-footers.

91. *Turning from a traverse, feet together.*

somewhat closer together calls for better edge control. He can consciously squeeze his knees and skis together in the turns (Picture 91).

But above all, he should stay with the concept of the connected turns and let nothing interrupt that idea.

The skier will find that the four-footers give him more of the "real ski" feeling. He has more chance to lean forward when he starts down steep slopes (leaning forward helps the balance at this point) and he will find that sitting back makes it easier to go through deep snow (Picture 92).

The four-foot stage should take another day or two. The idea is to push toward longer skis all the way through. The skier should not get *too* comfortable on his shorter skis, because there are rewards in going on to the longer ones: more speed, better ride, and faster runouts.

There are several bridging sequences to prepare for five-foot skis; the skier normally will go on to five-footers in two days.

There are, first, the different kinds of turns:

skier takes his four-footers out to a flat hard-snow surface and goes into the twist exercise (Pictures 87 and 88). The skis will have to be twisted harder, because the resistance of the four-footer is about twice that of the three-footer. This added resistance can be overcome by the skier only if he gives a real explosive twist, together with a little bouncing up and down as he brushes the skis back and forth on the snow (Pictures 87 and 88).

The skier who has trouble in twisting can use another skier's hands or his poles, as in the three-footer sequence, to get started. He then takes the four-footers down the slope (Pictures 89 and 90).

Again, he will have to bounce more and twist harder. He should think more than he has about twisting the skis farther, to give him braking power, because the four-footers are faster than the threes.

He should also think more about getting knees and skis together. This is the time to improve the edge control a bit, and getting the skis

92. *Turning on steep slopes with forward lean.*

93. *Turning with reverse on four-footers.*

The "comma position" is an easy way of weighting the outside ski. The knees bend in, the shoulders lean over the outside ski, and the skier takes the reverse position in the turn (Picture 93). The skier practices the comma in the turn to get weight on the outside ski.

If a skier skis weekends, sometime during the third or fourth weekend he will be ready to go onto five-foot skis.

94. *Turning in place on five-foot skis.*

twisting at ankle, leg, and waist. There is the one-ski twist.

Following the one-ski twist, the skier concentrates on getting the weight on the outside ski of the turn. This becomes important now. It is quite possible to ski four-footers without having the weight on the outside ski. But leaning on the outside ski is needed on the fives.

FIVE-FOOT SKIS

This starts, as with the other stages, by a twist in place (Picture 94). The resistance of the five-footers is considerably greater than the resistance of the four-footers. The skier *must* increase his twist force and start the turn quickly, explosively!

Once the skier can make ten or more turns in a row, back and forth in place, with the

95. *Continuous turns on five-footers, down the slope.*

96. *Sideslipping on five-foot skis.*

five-footers, he should go into sideslip practice to get the feel of flattening the ski (Picture 96). Then he should practice his bounce.

He must also try to work on his comma, so that he gets his weight to the outside ski in the turn. Otherwise, at the five-foot length, the skis will tend to cross or split. There is a very good exercise for this, and that is to lift the tail of the inside ski at the end of the turn (Picture 97). If the skier is good enough, he can lift the ski earlier and earlier in the turn, using more and more comma to do it.

Lastly, he should bounce into the turns. If he wishes, he can hop the tails just a bit to start the turn. The tip of the ski should stay on the snow, however.

The five-foot ski is a *real* ski. Not only are there wood five-footers available, but there are metal, Fiberglas, and wood fives made by Head, Shakespeare, and K-2 companies. The metal or Fiberglas ski is more expensive but inherently an easier ski than the wooden ski.

Progress from here on is up to the skier. He can try six-footers next, using the same methods to get a short turn, and then go on to sevens, if

five-footers, he can then take them down the slope. At this point, some skiers may have difficulty and should go back to the four-footers for another day or two. This is perfectly fine. The skier on four-footers can follow along with the skiers on five-foot skis. He will work up to five-footers eventually.

The five-footers should be used on the same easy slopes as the fours. The same concept of connected turns holds here (Picture 95). It is imperative that the skier work on his rhythm in the turns. Otherwise he will lose the valuable reflexes of the reverse motion he has built up and will lose the feeling for the short "wedel" turn. The turns on five-foot skis will not be quite as short because the skis are longer. But the turns should be made as short as possible. If the skier cannot make short turns, it is usually because he is *not* keeping the skis flat enough at the start of the turn and through the turn. If the skier has trouble making short turns on

97. *Getting weight on the outside ski.*

98. *Starting to edge in a turn.*

However, with a judicious bending-in of the knees, the skier can put his skis on edge through the last three quarters of the turn, increasing the amount of edging as the turn continues and achieving much more braking power (Picture 98).

The best way to practice bending-in, or "angulation," is to maintain the comma. The comma position has "reverse" shoulders and an inward bend at the knees (angulation). The more angulation, the more edging the skis get (Picture 99).

The reversed position of the shoulders makes it easier for the skier to bend at the waist as well. The bend at the waist is used to get the weight over the downhill ski. In the comma, the skier gets his weight on the outside ski solidly; otherwise the outside ski will slip and split away from the inside ski.

The other thing that the comma position introduces is the idea of "lead ski." The inside ski must be advanced about six inches. This keeps the inside ski from crossing the outside ski. The tip of the "following (outside) ski"

he is eager to try them. Each added length gives the skier better handling characteristics. But each added length also calls for more bounce, or lift, more weight shift to the outside ski, and more edge control.

Once the skier is on the ski that he feels is the right length for him, he will want to go on to steeper slopes.

The flat-ski "slewed" turn, which is what we have been discussing in these two chapters is not suitable for the steeper stuff. So, the skier has to learn to put his skis on edge.

EDGING SKIS

Edging means braking power, and braking power is what steep slopes call for.

It is important to remember here that the ski, even on steeper slopes, has to be flat at the start of the turn. It is edged later in the turn. You cannot twist to start an edged ski into the turn; start the turn with the skis flat.

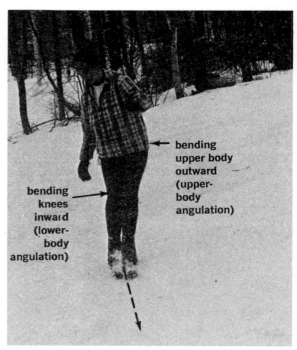

99. *Angulation to help edging.*

100. *Inside ski leading in left turn.*

101. *Inside ski leading in right turn.*

will hold the inside ski in place. It is clear that the comma or reverse position makes it easier to lead with the inside ski, because the reverse position causes the inside side of the body to advance.

This idea of "lead" ski is an essential part of turning. When turns are connected, there is a "change of lead." In a turn to the right, the right ski is inside and that ski leads. In a turn to the left, the left ski leads (Pictures 100 and 101). This keeps the skis from crossing in the turn.

The traverse position and the change of lead are introduced much later in the short-ski system than in other systems. In the first short-ski stages, the change of lead takes place almost automatically, because of the use of the reverse motion. On the five-foot ski, it does become desirable to change lead consciously. This is particularly so when the skier tries for the longer, carved turn. The longer the turn, the more likely the skis are to start crossing at the tip.

In Graduated Length Method, the skier stays away from the comma until he has really gotten the idea of connecting his turns. Once learned, the comma position is a stable position. The

102. *Traversing on five-footers.*

103. *Karl Pfeiffer of Head-Way.*

skier can also use it to traverse across any hill with admirable control, without sideslipping (Picture 102). It is a nice, easy thing to do—too easy, in fact. The skier will find that he wants very much to stay in this safe and stable position. The "traverse habit" or "traversitis" can become a major block to progress for the skier.

In the short-ski system, until the very end, then, he doesn't worry about traverse. He uses a series of slipping turns to get across the hill. He thus avoids, nearly always, the risk of catching "traversitis."

LATER GLM METHODS

There have been wide ripples from the original Taylor GLM school at Hogback, Vermont. Clif Taylor himself has subsequently taught at Squaw Valley, California, and now teaches at Loveland, Colorado; both places have GLM schools. Some schools like Vail, Colorado, have designed a "conservative GLM," using five-foot skis and a "wide track" approach still very much in the tradition of "direct turning," twisting the skis rather than letting them come around by themselves in passive turns.

However, by far the most important impetus behind GLM has come from the Head Ski Company.

THE HEAD-WAY METHOD

The first serious attempt to transplant GLM from Hogback, Vermont, came when, at the urging and with the aid of *Ski Magazine*, Karl Pfeiffer of Killington, Vermont, adapted the Taylor method to the five-day Killington Learn to Ski Week. This meant eliminating one step (the four-foot step) of the Taylor method and condensing some of the teaching; but the great advantage that this offered was a definite "package," including a time limit, a certain measured amount of instruction, and the skis necessary for the method—all at a given price.

The Killington GLM was so successful in attracting skiers that the Head Ski Company decided to back GLM by producing a series of

fall line

104

105

106

104 to 108. *Turn from a shallow traverse.*

fall line

turn from fall line

107

108

Head skis of the required lengths. They also hired Karl Pfeiffer to run a program they named "Head-Way," essentially the Killington GLM system sold on a franchise basis to selected ski schools.

The first step in Head-Way is not a twist on three-foot skis, but a back-and-forth hop on three-footers (very much like the Foeger system, see Chapter 6). Once he can hop the skis back and forth, the Head-Way skier learns to do uphill christies from a shallow traverse (Pictures 104 to 106).

He makes christies from steeper and steeper traverses until he can make fairly long turns across the fall line (Pictures 107 and 108); he also continues to make short back-and-forth turns, more like those the Taylor system uses exclusively.

From the three-foot ski, the Head-Way skier goes directly to a five-foot ski, skipping the four-foot stage for the sake of shortening the learning process. He learns to hop these back and forth first in place and then going down the hill. Then he learns the longer turns, the christies, as well as the short turn. On his fifth day, or sixth day if he chooses to keep on taking lessons, he should be able to go onto a six-foot ski length and repeat the process of short turns-long turns.

THE SPREAD OF GLM

There is a very definite ferment in American ski schools today, and it centers around GLM. Some of the leading schools have already adopted Head-Way, such as the Waterville Valley, New Hampshire, school run by Paul Pfosi (Picture 109). Pfosi plans to use Head-Way with the four-foot ski, as in the Taylor method.

Jerry Muth's ski school at Vail, Colorado, is trying to hit neatly between radical GLM methods such as Taylor's and the current American system. Muth's wide-track GLM (Picture 110) with five-foot skis is attractive to schools not yet ready to go all the way to the small three-foot or four-foot skis.

Not since the introduction of the Austrian shortswing (Chapter 5) has the way Americans are taught skiing been undergoing a greater change. And the changes will accelerate. The main thesis of all the new approaches is a simplified ladder to success: teach fewer turns; get the skiers moving, teach a single turn rather than teaching many different kinds of turns.

RENTING SHORT SKIS

Most GLM schools have their own stock of skis. This solves the problem of the skier's getting short-ski lengths for himself. In some other circumstances, he will have to supply his own

109. *Paul Pfosi of Waterville Valley, New Hampshire, teaching GLM.*

110. *Jerry Muth of Vail, Colorado, teaching GLM.*

lengths of short skis. Some rental shops at the various ski areas have a stock of varying lengths. But the skier may have to *buy* his own. This makes it somewhat more expensive by the time he is all the way through to six- or seven-foot skis, but he gains time, which is also worth money. Skiers who have outgrown their shorter skis often sell them or lend them to friends who want to start out. There is a seller's market in short skis today.

USING POLES

At some point in the GLM sequence, the skier should start using poles. This should come when he has confidence in making connected turns without the poles; having reached that stage, he will not use the pole to stop himself or to "pry" himself into the turn. "Hanging on the poles" to force the turn to start can be a major beginner's problem. But once the skier can take his poles along without letting them interfere with his skiing, they are a decided advantage. They act as extensions of the arms, giving the upper body more stability and making it easier to turn the feet *more* and the upper body *less*. Poles are very nice to rest on and to use when the skier is walking across the flat or climbing.

The skier uses the pole to "mark" the turn, jabbing the pole into the snow lightly when he starts his bounce to unweight the skis. When he goes on steeper slopes, he uses the pole more heavily, planting it hard and "riding over" the handle to help him get unweighted quickly. (See Chapter 10 for the exact form of planting the pole.)

SUMMING UP GLM

A skier who takes a GLM approach to parallel turns will have a number of things going for him.

First, he learns parallel from the beginning, or at least from nearly the beginning. He does not have to unlearn a stem-turn habit ingrained from long practice.

Second, he is going to get hurt less: statistics show the short ski is safer for beginners. A stem-turn skier has the highest incidence of injury in the sport.

Third, there is constant reinforcement of the skier's will to succeed. He will, on the average, get on a lift within sixty minutes or so of first putting on skis, and he will put miles of skiing under his belt the first day. This is not true of a stem skier.

By the end of a week or so, he will have found his proper length of ski for his first year of skiing. When he gets on a ski that is too long he will know it, because he won't be able to handle it on the terrain that he's been used to skiing. Therefore, he will never be saddled with a ski so unhandy that it deters him from skiing.

The GLM goes easily into the American system taught by most schools. A GLM skier with two weeks of skiing behind him should have no trouble taking a beginning parallel class in any American system school.

The skier will eventually learn the more rigorous snowplow and stem and stem christie turns; they have special application in situations such as narrow corridors, carrying a backpack, going at very slow speeds between skiers, etc. But by this time, the GLM skier is in no danger of being permanently stuck at the stem-turn level of skiing.

Until he gets good enough to ski on a six- or seven-foot ski, the GLM skier may take some kidding from other skiers. This may or may not be a factor weighty enough to deter a given skier. For some reason, a long ski is supposed to symbolize superior skiing. For sure, length has little to do with ability when you have the skier starting on long skis instead of graduating to them.

THE GLM SCHOOLS

The skier today has a choice of different kinds of GLM. Just to make my own conclusion clear, I will say the Taylor system, three- four- five- six- and onward to seven-foot skis, is the surest of the GLM systems. The danger of Head-Way is that skiers will drop out at the big critical jump from three- to five-foot skis. But Head-Way has the advantage of compactness and rapidity.

The "conservative" GLM schools are hedging. If you accept the premise that short skis are easier, then you have very little defense against going to three-foot skis, other than the resistance of instructors who have never skied on such short skis to teaching pupils on such short skis. Eventually, the three-footer will be the standard ski for the first-day skier.

There is a very good GLM film available for viewing. Any legitimate civic group or ski club can write Head Ski Company in Timonium, Maryland, and ask for a copy of *Five Days to Ski*. The writer directed this film and Karl Pfeiffer was the instructor. The film was shot by Summit Films, which is the Denver company that did *The Outer Limits, The Moebius Flip,* and *The Great Ski Chase,* all modern classics of ski filming.

Five Days to Ski is *cinéma vérité:* ten non-skiers learning to ski in front of the cameras showing the spills and frustrations together with the triumphs. It is the first film in which skiers were caught in synchronized sound, talking (or yelling) while they skied. It is a convincing document.

GLM SCHOOLS IN THE UNITED STATES

California

June Mountain Ski School
% Tex's Sporting Goods
June Lake, California 93529
  Head-Way area

Squaw Valley Ski School
Box 2278
Olympic Valley, California 95730
  Resort's own system

Colorado

Keystone International Ski School
Dillon, Colorado 80435
  Head-Way area

Loveland Ski School
Box 455
Georgetown, Colorado 80444
  Taylor system

Vail Ski School
Box 7
Vail, Colorado 81657
  Resort's own system

Aspen Highlands Ski School
P. O. Box T
Aspen, Colorado 81611
  Taylor system

Maine

Sugarloaf Mountain Ski School
Kingfield, Maine 04947
  Head-Way area

Massachusetts

Bousquet Ski School
Pittsfield, Massachusetts 01201
  Head-Way area

Egon Zimmermann Ski School
Blue Hills
Boston, Massachusetts, 02109
  Head-Way area

Michigan

Don Thomas Sporthaus Ski School
6600 Telegraph Road
Birmingham, Michigan 48010
  Head-Way area

New Hampshire

Waterville Valley Ski School
Waterville Valley, New Hampshire 03223
  Head-Way area

New Jersey

    Great Gorge Ski School
    McAfee, New Jersey 07428
      Head-Way area

New Mexico

    Taos Ski Valley Ski School
    Box 856
    Taos, New Mexico 87571
      Resort's own system

New York

    Greek Peak Ski School
    R.D. #2
    Cortland, New York 13045
      Head-Way area

    Gore Mountain Ski School
    North Creek, New York 12853
      Head-Way area

North Carolina

    Sugar Mountain Ski School
    P. O. Box 369
    Banner Elk, North Carolina 28604
      Head-Way area

Ohio

    The Ski Haus Ski School
    12413 Cedar Road
    Cleveland Heights, Ohio 44106
      Head-Way area

Pennsylvania

    Seven Springs Ski School
    Champion, Pennsylvania 15622
      Head-Way area

    Ski Roundtop Ski School
    R.D. #1
    Lewisberry, Pennsylvania 17339
      Head-Way area

Vermont

    Bromley Ski School
    Box 368
    Manchester Center, Vermont 05255
      Head-Way area

    Hogback Mountain Ski School
    Marlboro, Vermont 05344
      Taylor system

    Killington Ski School
    Killington, Vermont 05751
      Resort's own system

Chapter 5

WEDEL: SHORT TURNS ON LONG SKIS

How the Austrians started a revolution and how we use it today to control six- and seven-foot skis

Something as radical as GLM doesn't turn up out of the void: i.e., the ground had been prepared for it by wedel.

The history of the wedel turn is twenty years old. In the 1950s, the official state examiner for Austria's ski instructors, Dr. Stefan Kruckenhauser, introduced a new approach to skiing. The Kruckenhauser theory arrived in the United States in the ski press and a few years later, it was all over but the shouting. The official Austrian system was victorious through the length and breadth of the United States.

Professor Kruckenhauser arrived at his new theory by analyzing movie footage of ski racers. He was fascinated by the so-called "delayed shoulder turn" of racing technique. To Kruckenhauser, delayed shoulder foreshadowed an entirely new technique in recreational skiing.

The "delayed shoulder" was a product of slalom racing. This is an event in which a skier makes a number of very tight turns, one right after the other, to get through a series of paired poles, or gates. In most slalom turns, it is an advantage for the racer to get as close to the inside pole of the gate as he can.

Rotation limited the quickness with which one turn could follow another; it also limited how close one could get to the inside pole (Picture 111). Skiers started using the delayed shoulder and got closer to the proper pole. The delayed shoulder consisted of holding *back* the outside shoulder of the turn rather than thrusting it *forward* as in rotation. Holding the outside shoulder back and bending at the waist (which was made easy by holding the shoulder back) allowed the skier to brush the pole with his back (Picture 112).

Slalom gates are often set first to the right and then to the left. So, what was happening was this: the left shoulder was "delayed" at one gate and the right shoulder would be delayed at the next. The upper body was thus turned from side to side in the direction opposite the ski tips. The upper body turned in a direction opposite to that of the tips each time.

A little reflection convinced Kruckenhauser that the mid-body muscles were turning the upper body back and forth and were, as a result, *twisting* the skis *into the turns*. In other words, the racer no longer used *rotation* to start the skis into the turn, but used a series of connected "delayed shoulder" motions. Kruckenhauser had changed the name of the motion to "reverse shoulder" and announced that it *had replaced rotation*.

111. *A skier rotating his way around a slalom pole. Note that he isn't going to be able to get his skis very close to the pole because his left shoulder is at the pole and won't allow the skier to go any closer.*

112. *A skier reversing his way around a slalom pole. Note that the "delayed" outside shoulder lets him sneak the inside shoulder past the gate even though his skis are much closer to the gate than those of the skier in Picture 111. Also, he hits the pole with his back and slides off the pole, whereas, if he hit squarely with his shoulder, he might get hung up on the pole.*

113. *The comma position in parallel turns.*

The new position created a "looking downhill" appearance. The knees were bent toward the slope, there was a bend at the waist, and the outside shoulder was back. It was soon dubbed "comma," because it did look a bit like that punctuation mark (Picture 113).

The comma in the snowplow position was not quite as pronounced, but it was there (Picture 114).

The comma could easily be seen in the best racing skiers (Picture 115).

But there was a distinction here that the Austrians were not often careful to make. The difference was between the reverse *position*, or comma, and the reverse *movement*, or twist-turn.

If the reverse position is assumed with a slow motion, the act doesn't have any effect on the skis. It won't "kick" the skis into a turn. It does, however, give the skier a good comma position from which to edge the skis and get the weight in the outside ski, both essential to good skiing.

COUNTER-ROTATION

Another name for reverse is "counter-rotation." The American system uses this word for it. It is unfortunate, however, that the names for the new turn called attention to the shoulder and upper-body motion. It is the fast twist of the lower body and the *skis* into the turn that counts. It actually does no good to swing the shoulders in the reverse movement—unless the skis can respond in the opposite direction. The lower-body motion is being more and more stressed via Graduated Length Method and "direct turning" methods.

Kruckenhauser set up a system designed to teach first of all the upper-body reverse movement. The idea was that the skier could learn later to do it rapidly. The Austrian system of the 1950s required skiers to adopt the reverse position as early as the snowplow turn.

114. *The comma in a stem turn.*

115. *Comma position in a race. Jean-Claude Killy, one of France's greatest all-time racers, angulates and reverses as he goes through a gate, forming a comma position with his body.*

116. *A heel thrust starts a carved parallel turn.*

The beginner was taught to assume the comma position and go into the plow and stem turns. These turns, from beginning to end, are powered by S and G forces alone. They don't need any "kick."

About halfway through the Austrian system, Kruckenhauser introduces "heel thrust." First at this point, without specifying it, the Austrians were teaching reverse turning *to actually turn* the skis.

A heel thrust is a very short, fast, compact uphill christie. It is, in effect, a shove of the tails downhill from a traverse. As we have seen, a shove or hop of the tails is equivalent to a twist of the whole ski.

DOWN-UNWEIGHTING

The heel thrust, then, is used to turn from a traverse into a shallower traverse, just as the uphill christie is used. In Picture 116, the skier does a heel thrust by making a quick reverse at point (1), thrusting the skis downhill to point (2). What makes the thrust possible is a fast, reverse motion (3) and a dropping motion (4), which takes the weight off the skis momentarily. The skis then turn to a shallow traverse (5).

To most people, the "drop" or "down-unweighting" was a big innovation. It was an unweighting by a means not yet previously defined. Up to that time, all unweighting had been thought of in terms of a hop or an up-motion.

Yet, the theory of the down-motion unweighting is sound.

If you stand at full height and then drop your height several inches by doing a quick knee bend, the weight is momentarily taken off your feet. For a split second it is like the sudden starting down of an elevator. The period of weightlessness on skis makes it possible for the skier to twist the skis, or to put it another way, to thrust the heels of the skis to the side.

Down-unweighting and simultaneous heel thrust did not occupy nearly as much space in the Austrian books as the reverse position, yet it constituted the real Austrian revolution.

The quick little drop and thrust, combined with edging, made the racers of Austria successful. It was not so much the delayed shoulder as the quickness of the heel thrust that got them through the slalom gates so fast. However, it was the shoulders that got the attention.

HEEL THRUST AND WEDEL

The heel thrust can be used to carry the tails of the skis across the fall line into a shallower traverse. The motion is the same—drop and reverse (Pictures 117 and 118).

A heel thrust from a shallow traverse is an uphill christie. A sequence of such short thrusts with the heel—first a thrust across the fall line to the left and then a thrust across the fall line to the right—is the basic ingredient of both

117. *Running.*

the Austrian slalom racing style and the famous civilian version of it, the "wedel."

In the wedel, the skier makes a series of short turns back and forth across the fall line, thrusting the tails of the skis back and forth to do it. The shoulders move back and forth a bit but, in short turns, the shoulder motion is hardly noticeable. The optical illusion is that the legs

118. *Turning with down-unweighting.*

119. *First turn of a wedel series.*

120. *Second turn of a wedel series.*

thrust the skis first to one side and then to the other as the body stays motionless between.

In Picture 119, the skier has just made a wedel turn to the reader's left by pushing his ski tails to the right to point (1) in a heel thrust. This is immediately followed by a heel thrust to the right to point (2), starting a left turn (Picture 120). One follows the other without pause, giving a snakelike look to the series of turns.

This series of heel-thrust turns to alternate sides can also be thought of as a series of "twists" as in the Taylor method. The result of twisting the skis and of continuous heel-thrusting to alternate sides is the same.

The short parallel turn gives good control once the reverse motion (or heel thrust) has been learned.

THE CARVED TURN

As a parenthetical observation at this point, note that the mark of the real expert is not the short turn, which a lot of beginners now teach themselves, but the "carved short turn."

The "long carved turn" starts with a reverse (or in some cases with rotation) to set the skis at an angle to the original path. This turning power lasts only a second or so. Then, since the skis are edged to keep sideslipping to a minimum, the G and S forces take over to finish the turn. The skier rides these G and S forces the rest of the way around the turn, using enough edging (carving) to give him a powerful, smooth, long arc with little loss of speed (Pictures 121 to 123). This is not an easy turn, because if you edge too much in the last or passive part of the turn, the turn stops cold.

The wedel turn can be carved (made as a "short carved turn") by the expert. Note how much the ski is on edge at the end of the turns shown in Picture 120, where the skier is using a comma to give the skis lots of edge.

The carved wedel turn is a much more precise and powerful turn than the flat-ski or "slipped" wedel.

121 to 123. *A long carved parallel turn.*

However, a beginning skier *does not* have the edge control to do a *carved* wedel turn, and so he does a flat-ski wedel. This keeps him happy. If he is made to carve his turns from the beginning, he will be very unhappy, be-

cause edge control of the precise sort needed for carved turns takes endless practice.

THE SLIPPED TURN

The beginner on long skis should use the short "slipped" parallel turn with the skis somewhat apart and quite flat all the way through. This turn is what most self-taught parallel skiers use, operating on fairly hard, smooth snow. And it works.

The short slipped parallel turn is looked upon with disdain by some instructors. They say that such a turn is merely "turning the feet." Precisely. The beginner getting into parallel finds this method a lifesaver. The distance between the skis has the same effect as a "canted boot." It keeps the skier's weight "off the outside edge" of the skis. (Catching the outside edge is what commonly trips him in a turn.) And so he can get by with less precise edge control, since his wide stance already gives him a natural tendency to edge correctly.

The self-taught parallel skier confidently slews

124. Schmieren *turn.*

his skis back and forth and maintains pretty good control (Picture 124). Note the absence of comma position, which results in absence of edging, i.e., a flat ski.

Here we come to the fact that some methods, including the American system and the Foeger system, teach the carved turn to beginners. Graduated Length Method skiers have the advantage of learning the flat ski, short turn first and of having continually better control through the learning process.

It may be argued that the skier who learns via Graduated Length Method or who teaches himself the slewed short turn may never get to the long carved turn. On the other hand, if he doesn't learn the short flat turn, he may never learn to ski parallel at all.

The "slewed" wedel is also called *schmieren,* which is a German word meaning "to smear." Slewing is, in essence, a smearing of the skis back and forth. It works pretty well as a way of controlling speed on hard-packed, fairly smooth snow, and this is the condition of the snow on which most skiers ski today.

Every skier *should* learn to *schmieren* first. Then he will have a better chance to eventually learn the graceful, long carved turn.

Stein Eriksen, head of the ski school at Park City, Utah, is the master of this kind of turn. He has made it his trademark. The long carved turn with lots of reverse and angulation is still called the "Stein turn."

To summarize this chapter:

The Taylor twist and the Kruckenhauser heel thrust are sisters under the skin. The Kruckenhauser heel thrust was a way to make the long ski turn rapidly, almost in its own length, by means of a good hard reverse and a "drop" or down-unweighting.

Clif Taylor borrowed this for his short-ski system, enabling the average beginning skier to turn quickly.

The self-taught parallel skier senses that the short heel-thrust turn is the thing for him and he manages to approximate it very aptly with a *schmieren.*

Before we go on, a review of words used:

carved turn—a turn with the skis edged quite sharply through the latter part of the turn.

slipped turn—a turn with the skis flat on the snow through the whole turn.

down-unweighting—taking the weight off the skis with a drop motion. The skis stay on the snow.

reverse shoulder—the drawing back of the outside shoulder of the turn, and the advancing of the inside shoulder. Used to be called "delayed shoulder."

heel thrust—a fast, compact parallel turn, done with a short but powerful reverse motion. When done across the fall line, to both sides alternately, it is *schmieren,* very like the Taylor twist. When it has more edging to it, it is, for all practical purposes, the famous Austrian wedel.

schmieren—flat-ski wedel, short parallel turn typical of the self-taught skier and the GLM short-ski system for beginners.

wedel—series of short, continuous parallel turns with no traverse between them.

Chapter 6

THE FOEGER SYSTEM

A system of parallel turning on six- and seven-foot skis from the beginning

Now we come to the original "direct parallel." Walter Foeger's system has been copied (with Foeger's approval) in many schools in the East. Foeger conducts his own certification of instructors for these schools (the "American Parallel Technique" as Foeger now prefers to call it), just as the Professional Ski Instructors of America do for the American system.

Foeger is one of the genuine innovators in the history of ski-school systems and his system has been going as long as the American system.

125. *Walter Foeger in a parallel turn.*

126. *Picking up one ski—a Foeger exercise.*

There has been an obvious underground reaction between the two.

Foeger's method, like Head-Way, is built around the five- or six-day "ski week," in which skiers on vacation have lessons every day. By the end of this time, skiers who can take the concentrated teaching achieve a level of competence beyond that of a skier who takes scattered lessons.

Foeger divided his system into eight stages. The bridging sequences are worked out in detail. All American parallel schools follow them quite closely.

THE FIRST STAGE

Foeger's first stage, basic exercises, number about thirty. Not all the exercises are used by every Foeger teacher in every class. The exercises are there if the teacher feels that the skiers need it.

The objective of the first stage is balance and familiarity with the skis.

First, the skier stands in place, lifts one ski tail, then the other. He bends at the knees, straightens. He hops the tails of both skis. (This is a preparation for unweighting.) He swings one ski out to the side, holds the ski horizontal, and balances on the remaining ski. (This is a preparation for skating.)

The skier will now start running straight down the slope (known as schussing). For his first run, the skier simply lets the skis come to a stop naturally at the end of the run. Then he makes another schuss, picking up the tail of one ski and then the other as he runs (Picture 126). Next, he skis down while bending and straightening the knees. Then he skis down while using the bending and straightening motion to hop both tails off the snow.

One effect of these excellent sequences is to keep the skier "loose" while skiing down the

127. *Skating exercise.*

128. *Billy Kidd making a skating-step turn in the Stowe 1966 National races.*

hill, a thoroughly good idea. Too many skiers freeze into a rigid position depriving themselves of the chance to make quick movements to adjust their balance for the jolts of the terrain. One of the essences of skiing is to stay loose enough to react gracefully.

The straight running position of the Foeger skier is fairly erect. Foeger called it "resting on the bones." It means that, in the erect position, the skeleton takes the weight of the skier down through an erect backbone to the hipbones and down to the skis. The skier who hangs his upper body forward, obviously, is putting a great strain on the muscles of the back if he stays that way all the time.

129. *Traversing.*

THE SKATING STAGE

Foeger's second stage is called skating. Foeger said, "Skating under the instruction of a good teacher develops a tremendous amount of edge control, an understanding of change of direction and timing."

In Foeger's system, the skier first skates on flat ground. This is not hard; the skier who makes up his mind to it, can do it. He has

130. *Picking up one ski, hopping both skis, and then picking up one ski.*

131. *Start of tail hop clockwise.*

twist
upper body
to face left

original ski
positions

hop in
circle
to
left

132. *First hop in tail hop clockwise.*

to launch himself over one ski, go forward with it in one direction, then point the other ski off a bit, and go forward with it in a slightly new direction. He then does the same down a gentle slope that has a runout at the end. Next, instead of skating down the hill, he skates across the hill, skating up onto the higher ski, bringing the other ski up parallel, and then stepping up again onto the higher ski. The exercise in a skating-step turn (Picture 127).

Foeger pointed out that this exercise teaches the skier to "change edges." That is, the ski that the skier steps onto will naturally have the outside edge of the ski into the snow. As he steps off this ski, he will roll onto its inside edge, to give him enough traction to push.

This *rolling* of the ski from one edge to a flat position and then onto the other edge is an important phase of edge control: the good skier can feel just which edge is biting or when the ski is flat.

THE TRAVERSE

The Foeger traverse is quite like the American method traverse (Chapter 7) except that the skier's arms are held out a bit wider. The skier has a comma: reversed position, together with a leaning out from the knees and waist (Picture 129).

The skier now does the traverse exercises; he lifts the tail of one ski, lifts the tail of the other ski. Then he hops both ski tails off the snow. He then does these things in succession in the same traverse (Picture 130).

These moves create the ability to handle the skis separately and to move while in the traverse position. Skiers in a traverse should not freeze into a "picture position"; they must be able to move to correct for changes in speed and terrain.

133. *Start of tail hop counterclockwise.*

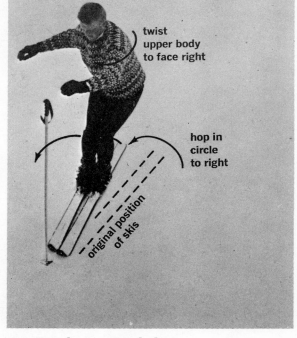

twist
upper body
to face right

hop in
circle
to right

original position
of skis

134. *First hop counterclockwise.*

PREPARING TO TURN

The "preparation turn to the mountain" is the crucial Foeger stage. Here the Foeger school introduces the reverse motion in earnest, together with a hop or unweighting motion.

The skier sticks a pole in the snow and stands with the tips of the skis at the pole. He then hops the tails of the skis to the left until he has at least partly circled the pole (Pictures 131 and 132). Then he does the same to the right (Pictures 133 and 134). As he jumps, he faces the direction of the jump, turning the upper body to do so.

This exercise does two things. First, it raises the idea of *direction* in the hopping of the tails; it shows the skier he can hop the tails to either side as well as straight into the air. Second, it

provides concentrated practice on the reverse motion. The upper body is turning one way while the skis are turning the other way. Hopping the tails to the left is, in effect, a movement that turns the ski tips to the right. Either way, it starts a right turn.

After doing it in place, the skier does the hop-and-reverse in motion; he hops tails downhill from a traverse run on an easy hill. He does it several times in rapid succession to make a sort of rough uphill turn or heel thrust.

Hopping the tails downhill to make the skis turn uphill is a sophisticated approach that most self-taught skiers won't arrive at by themselves. They strain to force the tips around instead, and that doesn't really work.

THE SIDE SLIDE

The Foeger system emphasizes next the side slide, as Foeger calls it, or the sideslip, as the

135. *Side sliding exercise.*

136. *Edging and sliding alternately.*

rest of the world calls it. Side sliding is just as important to the Foeger method as his more famous hopping exercises are.

Hopping the tails to one side without sliding is a very abrupt maneuver. The addition of the slide following the hop is what makes the hop valuable.

The side slide sequence is as follows.

The skier side-steps down the hill, so that he is facing bottom. Then he puts both poles behind him and pushes himself sideways down the hill (Picture 135). Then he tries it without using the poles, by flattening the skis.

The Foeger skier next does the "traverse side sliding." This means sliding sideways and forward, so that he is going across the hill as well as down.

Then there is "stair sliding," which is, first, side sliding and then putting skis on edge to make a short traverse (1 in Picture 136), and then another side slide (2 in Picture 136), and so on. This reminds the skier that he *must* consciously flatten the ski to side slide.

THE UPHILL TURN

The skier now starts on a moderate hill, takes a shallow traverse, and then hops in an "up-and-forward" motion, moving the tails of the skis downhill, with the reverse motion, landing the skis fairly flat, slides them around to the horizontal traverse position (Pictures 137 and 138).

Now he does the same for a steep traverse. Note how the skier crouches in Picture 137, comes up in Picture 138, and starts the tails turning in the air (or just brushing the surface of the snow). At the end of the turn, the skier's position is "reversed" and he is facing downhill (Picture 139). This is a rough form of heel thrust.

Next comes the short turn, which is closer to classic smooth heel thrust: more explosive reverse movement, smaller hop. There is the heel thrust from the shallow traverse (Picture 140). Then the skier makes the thrust across the fall line (Picture 141).

137

138

139. *End of the hop and slide turn.*

140. *Heel thrust to shallow traverse.*

141. *Short hop and slide with heel thrust.*

142. *Start of turn up the hill exercise.*

upper-body
quarter turn
hopping
tails
downhill

turn to come is
up the hill
or an uphill christie

143. *Reverse motion for turn up the hill.*

144. *Start of turn down the hill exercise.*

upper-body
half turn
hopping
tails
uphill

turn to come is
down the hill
or a full christie

145. *Reverse motion for turn down the hill.*

146. *Running, preparatory to long parallel turn.*

147. *Crouching, preparatory, to long parallel turn.*

148. *Skier comes up from his crouch.*

149. *Finish of the long parallel turn.*

150. *Stop turn from the fall line.*

151. *Two-hop turn through the fall line.*

All these started with a hop, or up-motion. This so-called "up-unweighting" is the way in which the Foeger system and the American system prepare for the heel thrust and uphill christie. In the Austrian reverse system, as we have seen, the heel thrust and the uphill christie are executed in a single down-motion, without any preparatory up-motion.

THE TURN DOWNHILL EXERCISE

In the uphill turn, the Foeger system has the skier on a traverse path, facing his tips, jumping the tails downhill as he reverses a *quarter turn* to face downhill (Pictures 142 and 143) but now in "preparation turn downhill," the basic exercise starts from a comma position with the upper body reversed (Picture 144). From this position, the skier jumps the ski tails uphill and reverses his upper body a *half turn*, to face the fall line (Picture 145).

After he can hop the skis with a half turn of the upper body the Foeger skier alternates a half turn left of the upper body with a half turn right. The tails hop left if the body turns left and so on; turning tails left, as we have seen, is equivalent to turning the tips right, thus, the motion left and right becomes very much like the Taylor twist. The difference is that the Foeger skier is hopping the full-length ski back and forth rather than twisting the short ski. But, in both the Foeger hop and the Taylor twist, the accent is on the actual *direct turning* of the skis.

THE TURN FROM THE FALL LINE

In Picture 146, the skier is coming down the slope in normal "running position." In Picture 147 he has crouched and is starting to come up. In Picture 148 he is up but has not yet started his skis turning. In Picture 149, he has spun the skis with a reverse motion and is headed for the horizontal traverse line. This is the Foeger turn from the fall line.

The Foeger skier first does a *stop turn* over a drop-off, to get a faster, better turn out of the fall line. The skier runs in the fall line and, with one hop and reverse (third figure from start in Picture 150), hops the skis part way around, and lets them slide the rest of the way, keeping his weight on the outside ski by means of the comma position. As the skis come around, the skier edges them more and more and finally edges them to a stop.

THE TURN DOWNHILL

Now we go on to the next step, in which the skier uses reverse upper-body motion combined with single hops of the tails uphill from a steep traverse.

Any time you hop the tails of the skis *uphill*, you are starting a turn *down the hill*. The uphill hop of the ski tails makes the ski tips swing decisively *down the hill*. This is the essence of the *turn down the hill*.

To make the "turn downhill" the Foeger skier turns the tips down the hill with a number of successive hops. Once he has it down to two hops (one *to* the fall line and the next one *across* the fall line) he is almost doing a full parallel turn.

In the final phase, the skier makes one hop of the tails from a steep traverse across the fall line, and the rest of the turn is slid (Picture 151).

This hop is then smoothed to fluid up-motion. The ski tails brush the snow rather than go off the snow. This is the final Foeger full parallel turn (Pictures 152 to 157).

What the skier can have at the end of a Foeger week is a long parallel turn on a moderate slope, with some capacity for shorter uphill christies and heel thrusts from the fall line.

Not every Foeger skier makes it this far in a week, but an amazing number seem to go a good deal of the way.

152

153

152 to 157. Full parallel turn from an initial traverse to the left to a new traverse to the right.

SUMMING UP THE FOEGER SYSTEM

Foeger's method works best with skiers who have had some skiing experience and who have not yet made it to the level of parallel skiing. The jolt provided by the somewhat acrobatic jump maneuvers at the beginning of the method is just the thing needed to stir the solid stem skier out of his stem habits.

For the average beginner, the Foeger method is too acrobatic; it is much more so than the GLM on three-footers.

The initial jump exercises on six- and seven-foot skis do wonders for the most co-ordinated 30 per cent of the beginners, and for the rest, Foeger represents a break-even situation, where there is some learning but not quite enough. If Foeger's acrobatics were cut down a bit and if Foeger were to use a ski at least as short as

five feet as a school ski, then the amount of learning would definitely increase.

As it is, Foeger represents a system that has had, in a direct way and even more, in an indirect way, a tremendous influence on the present American system in its parallel sequences. Further, the first Head-Way exercise is nearly identical to the first Foeger exercise.

Foeger's conception was brilliantly original. Foeger himself is obviously one of the few true innovators in the history of ski teaching. His teaching is at least 50 per cent based on the idea of "direct turning," which is today, in one form or another, the most powerful idea in ski teaching and likely to become more so. It is only in failing to recognize sufficiently the present fruitful trend toward a shorter ski and much simpler exercise sequences that Foeger has been less perspicacious than he was in his original ideas.

154

155

157

156

Chapter 7

THE AMERICAN SYSTEM: STEM TURNS

The system of the great tradition; what stem turns can do for the skier by controlling speed on six- and seven-foot skis

The American system is the "establishment," as far as American skiing goes.

The selfless devotion of a good many instructors in this country produced the organization known as the Professional Ski Instructors of America, which in turn produced the American system. Before that, we had the chaos system. Every school was a law unto itself, and there was no chance for good communication between the different United States schools. Now the American system is the common language of most of them.

Paul Valar, chairman of the technical committee, led the effort. Bill Lash of Utah was the first PSIA president and it was at his urging that the PSIA technical committee moved ahead. Other committee members were Willy Schaeffler, who ran our 1960 Olympics, Junior Bounous of Utah, and Max Dercum of Dillon, Colorado.

The founding of the American system led to a revolution in our custom of looking toward Europe for the guidance of experts. When wedel arrived, there was no over-all national U.S. body of ski teachers capable of evaluating the new idea. It took over on the force of Kruckenhauser's recommendation and the success of the Austrian racers.

158. *Paul Valar, head of the ski school at Cannon Mountain, New Hampshire, and of the Professional Ski Instructors' technical committee, was instrumental in the shaping of the American system of ski teaching.*

Today, in the face of a similar situation, the PSIA is in a position to evaluate any system by having certain ski schools work on it experimentally. This is the way Graduated Length Method is being tested today.

THE DOVETAILING SYSTEMS

All systems dovetail with the American system at some stage, because the primary goals of the American system are the long carved turn and the carved wedel. Both Foeger and GLM aspire to the same goals.

The American system, with its progress through snowplow, snowplow turn, and so on, is by far the most rigorous current method of attaining parallel skiing. Those who stick it out become thoroughly trained.

The stages of the American system are eleven in number. Each stage culminates in a "look" or "final form," the ideal way to finish out each stage. Naturally, the skier is not expected to *reach* the ideal in any one of these stages (it would take him too long to become that polished); only an instructor should be able to demonstrate the polished final form of each stage. This gives the skier a visible model to follow.

A good instructor is satisfied if the pupil is able to approximate the final form in any early stage. The instructor does not worry whether or not the skier is picture-pretty; he wants the skier to get on with it, to go on to higher stages.

The American system does not prescribe the bridging sequences for its ski schools. Individual ski school heads do that. This leaves a great deal of discretion to the schools. Within the freedom allowed them, then, the various PSIA schools have developed excellent sequences. Junior Bounous' Sundance school in Provo, Utah, is a good example of this.

Quite a number of PSIA schools use hop sequences like those used by Foeger. Other schools don't like the hop. These are typical differences in *method* among American ski schools; it should be stressed that the *technique,* or final form, is the same.

THE SNOWPLOW

The straight-running position is preliminary to the snowplow in the American system. It is a "tall in the saddle" look, with very little knee bend (Picture 159). The arms are relaxed and held close to the sides down to the elbow, with the forearm holding the poles out to the sides and in front just a little.

159. *Straight running.*

knee bend puts skis on edge

160. *Straight snowplow used as a brake.*

The second stage is the straight snowplow.

This is a braking maneuver, as discussed in Chapter 1. It also teaches the skier elementary edge control.

The edge control comes in when the skier wishes to control speed. He merely puts the skis more on edge. The edging is done with the bending-in of both knees as in angulation (Picture 160). The skier should stay quite relaxed and upright.

American system schools stress going from the running position into snowplow and back again. To do this, the skier in running position must "brush" the tails of his skis out to the sides as he moves forward. With too much edging, the skier won't be able to get into the plow. In closing the plow to the running position, the skier simply narrows the plow, squeezing his legs together.

The skier practices the snowplow on a gradual slope and gives himself plenty of time to stop. The snowplow is a slow-acting brake. Trying to make a fast stop will cause the skier to get into a cramped, over-edged position. The skier should not "freeze." He should bounce a bit as he goes down, bend the knees, straighten them, and so on. He should shift his weight back and forth so that he finds a comfortable posture for himself.

THE SNOWPLOW TURN

The third stage is the snowplow turn.

The snowplow turn is made from the fall line (Pictures 161 to 163). The theory is to increase the S and G forces on one ski by putting more weight on one ski. This ski becomes the steering ski. The S and G forces on this ski spin the skier around. Bending in the outside knee (the knee over the outside ski of the turn) and at the same time, leaning out over the outside ski with the shoulders is helpful. In the American system, leaning out at the shoulders is called "upper-body angulation." The bending-in of the knee is called "lower-body angulation."

In addition to angulation, the upper body assumes the reverse position (outside shoulder back) to help the skier to put more weight on the outside ski of the turn. The combination of reverse and angulation produces the American comma position.

The bending in of the knee is used to edge the ski on which the weight is, and consequently to give the ski turning and braking power. Proper edging of the ski (not too much to begin with) will give all the turning power necessary if the skier's weight is in the right place—just back of the center of the ski. There must be sufficient distance between S and G forces or the ski won't turn.

Once the skier can do one snowplow turn, he can do several in a row. At the end of one plow, since he is running in a traverse direction across the hill, he will have to turn from that traverse and come down into the fall line.

The final form of the snowplow turn is from the traverse direction (Picture 164). The skier holds the plow position as he traverses. Then he puts his weight on the *uphill* ski, and this ski becomes the outside ski at the turn and starts steering the skier toward the fall line (Picture 165). The skier keeps a fairly flat downhill ski at the beginning of the turn to get the turn started down the hill.

As the skier comes out of the fall line, he must edge the lower ski a bit more than at the beginning, so that he carves the turn and adds to its braking power.

The turn goes into the fall line and out again into the new traverse, going in the direction opposite the first turn (Picture 166).

The turn does not depend at all on a mid-body muscle movement. The S and G forces turn the ski.

THE TRAVERSE

The next stage in the American system is the traverse, or moving across the hill (Picture 167).

In the American system traverse, the skier sets his edges hard enough into the hill so that

161. *Snowplow turn: start.*

162. *Snowplow turn: weight shift.*

163. *Finish of snowplow turn.*

the skis do not sideslip. The edges are set by the comma position: the knees bend in toward the hill, the shoulders lean out away from the hill, and the lower shoulder is drawn back somewhat (Pictures 167 and 168).

The steeper the slope, the greater the bend at knee and waist. The skier must lean *down*

164. *Snowplow from a traverse: start.*

165. *Snowplow weight shift.*

166. *Snowplow finish.*

inward
knee bend
edges skis

167. *Traversing on an easy slope: front view.*

168. *Traversing on an easy slope: side view.*

upper body
leans out

extreme
inward
knee bend

169. *Traversing on a steep slope: front view.*

170. *Traversing on a steep slope: side view.*

173   **172**   **171**

171 to 173. Bridge to the stem turn: opening and closing the skis in a traverse.

the hill to make a good traverse on a steep hill even though this seems contrary to good sense (Pictures 169 and 170). Leaning out this way keeps the weight on the downhill ski, and as long as it's there, the skis will edge hard into the hill and the skis cannot split apart. If the skier gets too much weight on the uphill ski, it will "climb" up the hill away from him and disrupt the traverse.

The reverse that is used in the traverse is called "countermotion" in the vocabulary of the American system; it refers to the *relatively slow action of getting into the reverse position;* reverse is being used as a *position.*

THE STEM TURN

The next stage of the American system is the stem turn. The stem turn differs from the snowplow in that the stem starts in a traverse with skis together. In a snowplow turn skis are always in a "V" position. Then the skier moving in a traverse opens the uphill ski (or "stems" it) to assume stem position. The skier proceeds now as in the snowplow turn.

A bridge sequence most frequently used is the practice exercise of opening and closing the uphill ski while running in a traverse (Pictures 171 to 173). This prepares the skier for the stem turn because it teaches him to open the stem and close it.

The instant after the stem is made, he loads his weight onto the outside ski of the turn, and that becomes the steering ski. At the finish, when he comes back to a horizontal traverse, he closes the skis again and assumes the traverse position learned in the previous stage (Pictures 174 to 177).

In the stem turn itself, the skier goes from the traverse, stems his ski, and puts his weight on the upper, outside ski of the turn. This ski steers the skier into the fall line and out of the fall line again to complete the turn. At the end, the skier slowly squeezes the inside ski together with the outside. His main weight is on the outside ski all the way through the turn.

The stem turn requires the skier to cross the slope in the traverse position. (In the snowplow turn, he has to cross the slope in the stem position.) The quicker the turn, the more the control, of course. To speed the turn, the skier will "step" hard onto the stemmed ski as he stems it; the force of the weight shift onto the ski will help the turn to start right there. Needless to say, the more weight on the outside ski, the more turning power (the S and G forces

174 and 175. *The stem turn.*

original traverse

175

174

176

new traverse

177

176 and 177. *Finish of the stem turn.*

need weight to work well). The more turning power, the more rapidly the ski comes around through the fall line and into the safe, slow part of the turn coming out of the fall line to the shallow traverse.

A good skier can work into a stem turn in a few days, sometimes in a weekend. Others will have to stay with the plow for the weekend. In either case, the skier will have a serviceable turn for moderate slopes at the end of a couple of days, and this is the strength of the American system.

The skier ought to go onward soon. If he spends more than four or five weekends stemming, he will have formed a habit that is hard to overcome. He will have a difficult time bringing the skis together for parallel turns.

The skier with only the stem at his disposal is going to find himself on parts of intermediate trails that are too steep for him. This is the nature of ski trails and of skiers. *If* the skier had a good forward sideslip at this point, in addition to his stem, he could avoid the difficulty of the horror spot in the trail. He could sideslip right on down. This would be a boon to other skiers who are constantly being held up at difficult sections by the stem skiers who jam the trail and cannot sideslip the steep spots.

Thus, the next step in the American system concerns itself with the sideslip.

Chapter 8

THE FIRST CHRISTIE TURNS
OF THE
AMERICAN SYSTEM

The early christie turns and how they lead toward full parallel turns

To get into the sideslip, the skier stands in place on a steep slope, supporting himself by his poles on the uphill and downhill sides. The trick is to make the skis go flat and to slide from the upper pole to the lower pole. The knees must move away from the slope to flatten the skis, enabling the skis to sideslip (Pictures 181 and 182).

Once the skier has the co-ordination needed to flatten the skis, he starts off in a traverse (Picture 178), hops or straightens a bit, and flattens the skis as he lands (Picture 179). This starts him into a forward sideslip, in which he moves forward and down (Picture 180).

It is crucial for the skier to familiarize himself with the sideslip at this point in the American system. The next phases, and his own progress, depend on it.

The skier next does the *vertical* sideslip (Pictures 181 and 182). One further exercise: the skier starts the forward sideslip with a hop of the skis instead of with just an up-motion. This hop motion is the more vigorous unweighting action that will be used on steep hills. Thus, the skier starts the downhill slide with a full hop, rather than with just an up-motion.

This work on up-motion and hop is the first point in the American system at which unweighting is brought into play. It sets the stage for the unweighting motions that follow, in the parallel turns.

The skier who can both stem and sideslip has got a fairly good set of skills. He can handle most intermediate trails, sideslipping past such moguls and down such steeps as he does not care to make turns on. The sideslip gets the skier past places that his turning skill can't dispose of.

The other use for the sideslip is to help the skier to turn more easily. The skier who is having trouble getting his turn started down into the fall line from a traverse can often work wonders by going into a sideslip first. Once the skier is in a sideslip, the skis are already flat and dropping, a very gentle stem serves to start him into the turn.

THE UPHILL CHRISTIE

In the American system, the sideslip leads to the uphill christie.

The first uphill-christie exercise is practiced on the side of the hill, at a standstill. It is reminiscent of Foeger's hop and twist exercises on the flat. The ski tips stay at the same spot, marked in Pictures 183 and 184.

The skier stands with skis pointing across the hill. Then he hops and turns the upper body downhill. Next, he does the same thing with an easy up-motion rather than with a hop.

This is the first point in the American system at which the skier employs a *swift* reverse motion rather than using a slow reverse motion. In this bridge exercise to the uphill christie, the skier is actually spinning the skis with the reverse motion for the first time. In the American system, this reverse motion is called "counter-rotation."

The ski seems to have moved only at the tail but the result is a spin.

If the skier jumped straight up and made his reverse motion and then came down on the same spot, it would look just like the GLM twist (Picture 185).

The uphill christie, as used in the American system, requires a traverse (Picture 186), an up-motion (Picture 187), reverse to start turning; the skis come down fairly flat (Picture 188). The S and G forces finish turning the skis (Picture 189).

THE FAN SEQUENCE

We have reached the point in the American system now at which a few American ski schools introduce the famous "fan" bridging sequence. Most schools save the fan for a later time, after the next major turn, which is called the stem christie.

In the fan sequence, the skier starts out from a given point on the slope. He starts his first

forward side slip stops

180

run in a shallow traverse and makes an uphill christie (Pictures 190 to 193).

Then he makes a christie from a steeper traverse (Pictures 194 to 196), having started from the same point.

Finally, he makes a christie from the fall line (Pictures 197 to 200).

The ski tracks in this exercise fan out from the single starting point like ribs of a fan, giving the exercise its name. The objective of the fan is to make longer and longer sweeping turns from a steeper and steeper angle. This sweeping parallel from the fall line is the last half of the stem-christie turn, the next turn to come.

One American ski school makes an attempt to bypass the next turn, the stem christie, altogether. Look again at Pictures 197 to 200. They actually show a turn *across* the fall line rather than just "from the fall line."

forward sideslip

179. *Flattening the skis.*

original traverse

178. *Forward sideslip: the hop.*

skis on edge stay in place

181. *Start of a vertical sideslip.*

flat skis sideslip

182. *Flattening skis in the sideslip.*

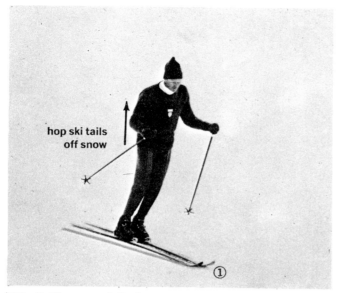

183. *Bridge to uphill christie: hop.*

184. *Upper body reverse is added.*

Joy Lucas of PSIA has written, "If you have pupils going down the fall line and turning their feet together, it is only a matter of minutes until they can be connecting a full parallel turn *across* the fall line . . . Why split their feet again just to teach them the stem christie?"

In other words, why not go right from here to parallel?

Ski schools which can bring this about—eliminating a whole turn (the stem christie)—could make the American system a great deal more compact.

186. *Uphill christie: crouch.*

187. *Uphill christie: hop.*

185. *Hop-and-reverse is like the Taylor twist.*

BRIDGES TO STEM CHRISTIE

Some American system skiers need the stem christie.

The stem christie is the combination of the stem with the uphill christie. The skier uses the combination in the following manner: he stems to the fall line and then "closes" the skis to parallel position after the fall line.

It is a stable turn.

Some skiers use the "stem-christie garland" as a bridge from the uphill christie to the stem christie. In this exercise, the skier starts off on a traverse, stems the uphill ski, unweights, and then closes the skis rapidly. The rapid closing motion sends both skis into an uphill christie (Pictures 201 and 202). A series of these is a stem-christie garland.

This procedure gives the skier practice in the up-unweighting and quick closing of the skis that occurs in the stem christie.

Other schools prefer to use the "snowplow christie." This is a turn in the fall line in which the skier starts out in a stem position and crouches. Then he up-unweights, closes his skis hard, and reverses with his down-motion. This gives him a fairly fast uphill christie turn out of the stem or plow position (Pictures 203 and 204).

The beginning stem christie starts in a stem; the stem is held until the skier turns into the fall line and is closed after that.

188. *Uphill christie: twist.*

189. *Uphill christie: slide.*

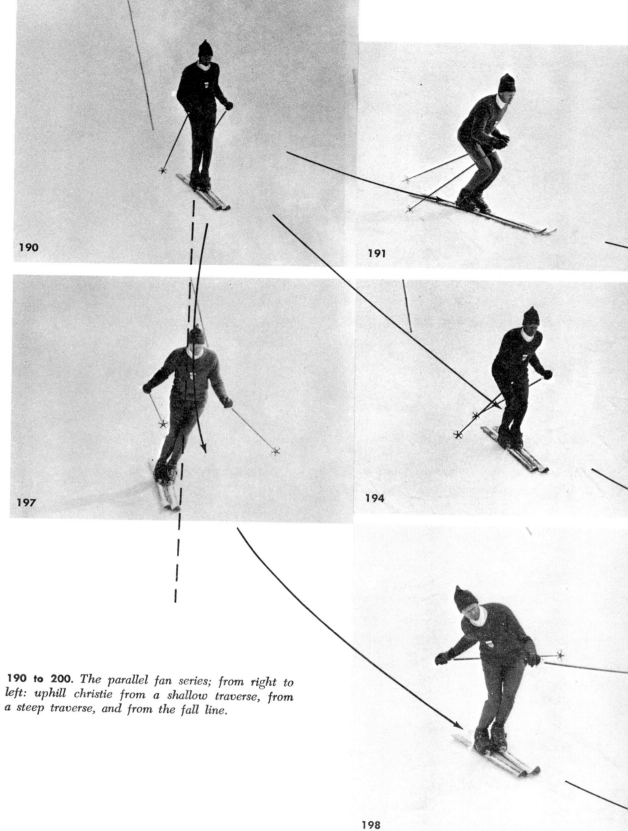

190 to 200. *The parallel fan series; from right to left: uphill christie from a shallow traverse, from a steep traverse, and from the fall line.*

190

191

197

194

198

193

196

200

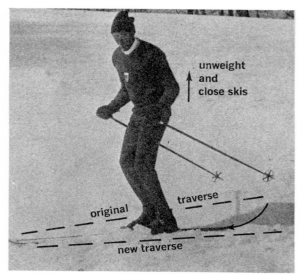

202. *Stem garland: finish.*

201. *Stem garland: start.*

In the final form, the stem christie is made from a shallow traverse, starting like the stem turn (Picture 205). In the fall line, the skier crouches, up-unweights, and brings the inside ski parallel to the outside, reversing to keep the skis turning. The skis are brought together before the fall line, so that the whole last part of the turn is a parallel turn (Pictures 207 to 210) using S and G forces.

Once the skier up-unweights and kicks the tips into the fall line with a reverse motion, the balance is "dynamic." That is, the weight is kept on the outside ski; the skier balances over it. If the weight goes on the inside ski at this point, the skis will split, and the turn stop.

The turn is stopped just as the uphill christie is stopped; at the end of the turn, when the S and G forces are turning the skis, the skier simply sinks and angulates to set the edges of the skis so that they stop turning; the stem christie is then complete.

The stem christie is a good, sturdy, and serviceable turn. The stem christie can be used on steep slopes to maintain control in the fall line.

Schools are now actively looking for short cuts to get skiers quickly into the stem christie, rather than spending much time on the stem. Once the skier is in the stem christie, the next step is parallel.

203

204. *Snowplow christie: finish.*

206

205

207

205 to 210. *The stem christie from the original traverse to the right to the new traverse to the left. Skier stems (206), up-unweights (207), and closes skis. S and G forces finish the turn (208 to 210).*

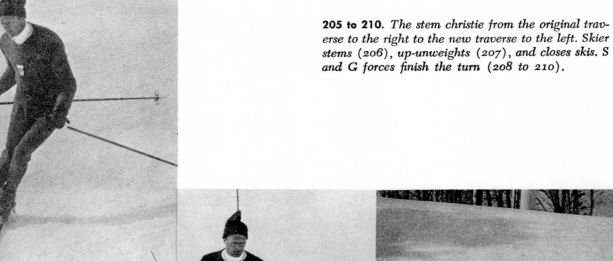

208

209

210

Chapter 9

ADVANCED AMERICAN TURNS

Parallel, wedel, and split rotation turns and how they are related

The parallel turn is the crown of the American system. By the time the American system skier reaches this point, he will be steady enough to make a reasonable parallel without suffering

214

from the speeds necessary to make it. The American system parallel is a long turn, it needs quite a bit of speed. In fact, the American system skier needs a couple of concentrated weeks to work into this stage. He has usually been skiing for at least one season, so he is relatively experienced.

The American system parallel comes in two parts: first, the parallel without check, and second, the parallel with check. The first is a swooping, effortless, graceful turn with a minimum of motion and a maximum of speed. The second, which involves the check or braking motion at the start of the turn, is for steeper slopes where

214 to 216. *Last half of parallel turn is finished by S and G forces.*

215

216

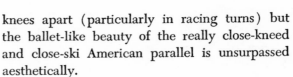

211. *Parallel without check: start.*

212. *Crouch before up-motion.*

213. *Up-motion and reverse.*

the skier needs to cut his speed before going on to the next turn.

A parallel is a turn without a stem movement. The skis are kept side by side and close together through the whole turn. The best form is with the knees fitted with the outside one behind the inside. Lots of skiers today ski with knees apart (particularly in racing turns) but the ballet-like beauty of the really close-kneed and close-ski American parallel is unsurpassed aesthetically.

BRIDGES TO PARALLEL

By the time he can do an advanced stem christie, the skier has a good sense of up-un-weighting *before* the fall line. A stem, in effect, is shoving the tail of one ski up toward the fall

219   218   217

217 to 219. *Beginning of parallel with check.*

222. *Up and over the pole.*

223

line. The stem-christie skier shoves *both* skis toward the fall line during up-unweighting.

The traditional way of bridging to parallel is to progressively reduce the size of the stem in the stem christie, and to close the stem earlier and earlier in the turn until there is just a little residual stem left at the beginning of the turn.

224

223 to 226. *Parallel with check is finished by S and G forces.*

225

221. *Crouch before up-motion.*   **220.** *Parallel with check: start.*

A second way of approaching parallel is to use the fan exercise. The skier starts with an uphill christie from a shallow traverse and works up to an uphill christie from the fall line. Finally, he does an uphill christie *across* the fall line. This is not so very far from the full parallel turn.

The full parallel first done in the American system is "parallel without check."

The skier starts on a traverse (Picture 211). Then he goes into a crouch (Picture 212), much as he does for the uphill christie. When he springs, he turns both ski tails uphill (Picture 213), shoving them toward the fall line. He reverses to thrust the skis into the turn.

From here on, the turn is a christie across the fall line, such as the skier has already seen in the fan exercise (Pictures 214 to 216).

PARALLEL WITH CHECK

The next step up—and the bridge toward the next step (wedel)—is the "parallel with check."

The skier who does a heel thrust and sets his edges with exaggerated angulation and reverse during a dropping motion of the whole body will bring his weight down hard on the edges and cause a sudden stop or slowing down. This is a check. It "sets" the skis.

The most generally used bridge to parallel with check is the "check hop garland." This is a form of practice for the very beginning part of the turn.

The skier goes on a traverse, makes a short heel thrust, sets the skis in a check, sets the pole in the snow on the down-motion, and then

226

hops the tails a bit up the hill, as if starting down into the turn. However, he does not make the turn. He lets the tails of the skis land and slide back to the traverse path they had before.

The skier makes a row of these "check hops" to make the check hop garland.

When the skier can make several check hops in a row without any trouble, he is ready for "parallel with check."

To make a parallel with check, the skier simply goes from a traverse (Picture 220) to a check (Picture 221), and then uses an up-motion to start the turn (Picture 222) down the hill. It is like an ordinary parallel from there on.

The parallel with check is the first form in which the American system skier really uses his poles.

It is very important that the skier should not use the pole wrongly. The pole is used to unweight. It thrusts the skier *upward*. It should not be used to "hook" the skier into the turn. It is planted close to the skis and the skier "rides over" the handle of the pole, using the reverse motion, not leverage from the pole, to swing the skis into the turn.

Parallel with check kills the skier's speed and makes it easy to turn on a small spot on a steep slope.

The remaining element for control on steep slopes is the short turn. And that comes next, with wedel.

WEDEL TURNS

There has been some confusion between short parallel and wedel. Technically, wedel is a series of short parallels without any connecting traverses. But there is such a thing as a short parallel turn by itself. Each short parallel, individually, can be called a wedel turn. But the word "wedel" by itself means a series of these turns.

Wedel is the last of the final forms in the American system. There are various wedels, from the very flat *schmieren* with no edge set, to normal wedel with some edging, to the hard-edged carved wedel, and on to the "hop wedel" for very steep slopes.

The flat-ski wedel is a bridge to the carved wedel and hop wedel used on steep slopes. The steep-slope wedels use short radius turns and hard braking edge work to keep the skier's speed under good control.

Each wedel turn is cut off and a new wedel turn started before the skis reach a shallow traverse angle.

BRIDGES TO WEDEL

Since there is so short a distance between turns, and since the pole has to be used to help unweighting, the pole action is fast. As soon as the skier has placed one pole and ridden over it to begin one turn, the other pole must be brought forward to be planted for the next turn.

One necessary bridge to wedel is a pole exercise. The skier goes down the fall line of a gentle slope and places first one pole and then the next, "walking" the poles down the hill. He passes the pole in each case without attempting to use it for unweighting (Picture 227).

Next, while doing the same thing, he uses the pole at each plant to make an up-motion, letting the tails of the skis come down straight (Picture 228).

He does the same thing again, except that he makes a heel thrust to the side away from the pole when he comes down (Pictures 229 and 230).

The sequence is "plant pole, hop, and heel thrust."

At the end of the heel thrust, he plants the pole for the next hop (Picture 230).

The skier first concentrates on making one wedel turn at a time. As he goes toward the "continuous turning" of wedel he starts putting turns closer together.

To arrive at wedel, the skier simply reduces the hop motion and makes it smooth and quick, a little up-motion, so that the tails of the skis do not leave the snow. Then he connects one turn

to the next, so that as soon as he comes out of one turn, he is going into another one.

When he gets the real feel of it, the skier will be thinking of it as a number of connected heel thrusts, with the thrust being made almost straight out to the sides from the fall line.

The skier, in effect, plants the pole and spins around it. In a very short space, the skier has turned the skis and is ready for the next turn, as shown in the turn simulated by a puppet model (Picture 231).

The wedel developed out of slalom racing and is still used extensively in such slalom configurations as a "flush" or series of gates set one above

227. Walking the poles.

up motion

planting pole

228. Lifting tails of skis.

229

229 and 230. *First turn of a wedel turn series.*

fall line

230

the other where the racer must make quick, consecutive linked turns. In Picture 232, a skier is shown entering between one pair of poles and he is planting his own pole to get set for a turn between the next pair of poles in a flush. At high speeds, this can get pretty exciting (Picture 233).

Short turns and continuous turning are the best defenses against steepness. There is every

231. *Polework co-ordinated with two wedel turns.*

reason to eliminate traverses between turns on a steep hill, if you want to control your descent properly. The skier may have to make a turn every half second or so on the steepest part if he really wants to keep his speed down.

When it comes to wedel, there are very small differences in the four major systems: Austrian, French, American, and Canadian. The down-motion and the up-motion stressed in one system or another at earlier stages blend into the up-down bobbing movement of the wedel. Up-unweighting and down-unweighting, consecutively, figure in the wedel.

In the long, parallel turns, however, there is a difference. The long parallel of the American uses an up-unweighting up-motion, where the Canadian uses a down-motion. The Canadian schools' reverse motion is definitely more subdued. The shoulders are held more "square" (not reversed as much) through the turn.

232. *Skier in a slalom "flush."*

233. *High-speed slalom.*

reversing
to finish
first turn

234

unweighting
before
reverse
motion is
finished

tips
kicked
into
second
turn

235

new
reverse
motion
finishes
second turn

236

234 to 236. *The split rotation turn.*

This, however, is the major difference in the Canadian schools in the United States. The Canadian Ski Instructors Alliance, headed by Ernie McCulloch, has instructors very much on a par with those of the American system, and there are no real differences (other than usual differences in "method") between the classes in the Canadian and the United States systems. In fact, the two systems are planning to merge. Their first joint meeting was at Vail, Colorado, in April 1970.

In the French parallel, which is taught in only one or two schools in the United States, there is a great difference. The French use a definite rotation rather than a reverse to start the long parallel turn.

SPLIT ROTATION

The skier who has finished his turn with an energetic reverse motion can do one of two things. He can absorb all this energy by setting his edges hard and *stopping* the reverse motion with a check. Or, he can start unweighting *before* the reverse motion is completely finished. In this case, the very last part of the reverse motion tends to *knock* the tips of the skis into the next turn as the reverse motion is slowed down and comes to a stop. This effect has been given various names—"tip pull," "pre-rotation," "split rotation," "anticipation."

The question arises whether the French keep some of their rotation movement in short parallel turns, i.e., when they wedel. The answer is, they do. This rotation blends with the normal United States-Austrian wedel and is helpful. Many good skiers from all systems use a little rotation to smooth up their wedel and make it more powerful. It's "split-rotation wedel."

When the wedel turn is finished in a heel thrust, as all good wedel turns should be, the reversing motion that ends the heel thrust *can* be carried over into the next turn as a rotation movement *into* that turn.

It works this way.

The skier who wants to use split rotation in

exaggerated rotation
toward turn
kicks tip into turn

traverse

237

skier
up-unweights
and starts
upper

body
reversing
in direction
opposite turn

238

finish of
reverse
motion in
mambo turn

239

237 to 239. *The mambo turn.*

wedel times his reverse (Picture 234) so that he is unweighting for his next turn, blocks as he ends the reverse motion of his turn (Picture 235). This blocking of the reverse motion kicks the skis into the next turn (Picture 236).

MAMBO

This brings us to mambo, an exaggeration of split rotation. The skier who wants to mambo simply does the split rotation and holds off blocking the initial rotation as long as he can.

The skier who mambos makes a full rotation of the upper body to start with and carries his lead arm over to the far side of his skis, as far as he can. Then, because the middle muscles can't stretch any further (Picture 237) the rotation is clocked or slowed down and the skis are pulled into the turn, provided the skier has the skis flat at that moment so they don't offer much resistance.

The skier now starts to reverse (Picture 238), which keeps the skis moving in the same direction. (A rotation to the right and a reverse to the left both tend to move the skis to the right.)

When his reverse ends, it has shot the skis around to the new traverse (Picture 239).

Mambo is lots of fun. It looks good, and it is a way of learning split rotation. But, in itself, it is more of an exercise than a useful turn.

NEW METHODS IN THE AMERICAN SYSTEM

There has been a recent move toward a whole new approach to the method of teaching the American system. Until now, the general idea has been to teach the classic ladder of steps, from snowplow through to parallel in that order. But today, these various turns are being condensed into what someone has called "a single crude turn." This turn may be a "wide track stem" or "open stem" (a stem with tips apart but closer to each other than the tails are to each other) (Pictures 240 to 242). Or, it may be wide track

240

241

242

240 to 242. *Wide track stem, or open stem turn.*

parallel, with skis the same distance apart at tips and tails but a foot or so apart.

The skier is encouraged to go out and make a *whole* turn, even if it is rough, even if the skis are spread apart. Parts of the turn, such as the traverse part, the uphill part, the downhill part, are not practiced except as in a whole turn. The skier, moreover, is encouraged to actively turn the skis and ignore the S and G forces. Make a short, snappy turn, in other words, and do it *now,* and do *another.*

Thus, GLM with its direct active turn has influenced long-ski teaching too, so that now the "direct turn" is the latest (and very healthy) cry in ski teaching method.

Part of the impetus for this condensation of the learning steps has come from Kruckenhauser himself. His new teaching method centers upon one turn, an "open stem" or *offener schwung* (Pictures 240 to 242). His wide-track, open-turn approach is combined with a five-foot ski.

MERGING SYSTEMS

The Canadian Ski Instructors Alliance has been working on the same thing.

In Pictures 243 to 246, Ernie McCulloch, head of the Canadian Alliance, shows how the *offener schwung* becomes a parallel turn. The skier starts in an open stem, and then, in the more advanced stages of learning the turn, he closes the skis at the end of the turn.

The Head-Way system uses a wide stance parallel turn. In Pictures 247 and 248, Karl Pfeiffer of Head-Way shows how the wide track parallel on five-foot skis becomes a normal parallel on six- and seven-foot skis.

There is an interesting comparison of open stem and wide track parallel in Pictures 249 to 252. Dixi Nohl of Madonna Mountain, Vermont, demonstrates the Kruckenhauser open stem beside Karl Pfeiffer's wide track turn on five-foot skis. The similarities are more notable than the differences. In effect, the new approach, the

243

244

245

246

243 to 246. *The open stem, a wide stance turn halfway between stem and parallel becomes parallel at the end.*

247

247 and 248. *Karl Pfeiffer of Head-Way in a wide track parallel turn.*   248

249

250

249 to 252. *The wide track parallel and the wide track stem together.*

251

252

253. *Alan Penz, recent world slalom champ, in a wide track racing turn.*

"rough turn" approach, is wiping out the distinction between parallel and stem, and is akin to the GLM turn, as well. Thus, all present systems seem to be merging.

The rough turns taught in the new Austrian method and in various U.S. schools are eventually refined so that they become nice, ballet-like American parallel turns.

Racing turns, however, are mostly now wide track. The old classic feet-together racing turn of the Austrians has given way to wider-track, wilder turns that brought the French to the top in recent years, as shown by Alan Penz (Picture 253), recent world slalom champion from France. In racing, wide track is here to stay.

SUMMING UP THE AMERICAN SYSTEM

The future of the American system lies in the present trend in the most advanced schools, such as Jerry Muth's in Vail, Colorado, toward de-emphasizing the stem sequences, in favor of a single crude open stem, quickly taught and quickly abandoned for a wide track parallel turn. From there on, the refinement of the parallel turn can fruitfully proceed along the lines of this chapter. Times have changed and most skiers no longer have the time or the inclination to undergo the rigors of the classic system, waiting several seasons before they become proficient parallel skiers. Indeed, the whole idea of the new sequences is to speed the skier into parallel, via a "direct turning" philosophy, in which the skier, with skis apart, consciously twists both skis, and makes them turn much as in Taylor's GLM.

As schools start getting into the habit of supplying short teaching skis, say five-footers, as Vail now does, then the American system and GLM will be on intercepting courses, to meet somewhere in the future, for the benefit of American skiers.

Chapter 10

SLOPE SAVVY

The problems of terrain and what the skier can do about them

Technique includes more than turning power and school turns. In addition to the challenge of the technique, there is the challenge of steep terrain.

This doesn't mean that the beginning skier should go out of his way to find challenge. There is nothing so detrimental to learning as a slope too steep to handle. Keep to the moderate slope at the beginning of the day if you are trying to learn some technique. You can then concentrate on form rather than on the slope. I have watched skiers fume because bad weather confined them to the easy slopes. But while they were confined to the easy slopes, they worked out bugs in their skiing. They finally had time to think about their faults.

But unfortunately, most trails designated as "intermediate" have a few *expert* spots. The same is true with most beginners' trails: they have intermediate spots in them somewhere.

And so, the challenge of steepness must be met early in every skier's life.

Steepness is, first of all, a psychological hazard. The skier tends to shy away, to lean in *toward* the hill on a steep slope rather than increase his lean *away* from the hill. The skier must, instead, lean out, over the downhill ski, which is the safe ski even if toward the steepness.

A second steepness problem is starting the turn down the hill with enough force. The skier who begins timidly finds himself "stuck." He *can* often get out, simply by going into a sideslip

and then making the turn. The very fact that the skis are moving down the hill sideways makes the turn down the hill easier, both psychologically and as a matter of engineering forces. But best make the first part of the turn *forceful*. Then one will not get stuck.

STEEP STEM TURNS

The stem skier must get his weight firmly onto the uphill ski, the ski he stems. It will help if he flattens the downhill ski as he starts to stem. He will thus slip down as he stems. A very little pressure on the uphill ski will start the turn into the fall line. If he makes the mistake of edging the downhill ski hard to keep the ski from slipping, he will not be able to turn downhill at all. The skier should therefore let the downhill ski sideslip and *then* make the turn.

The over-edging of the downhill ski is often the cause of the "refusal" of the skis to go into a downhill turn on steep terrain.

The skier must not overedge the uphill ski, either. If he does, the ski will tend to "track" rather than turn. He should start the edging with a small angle to the snow and increase it with a slow inward bend of the ankle and the uphill knee as the turn starts. Once across the fall line, the skier can then edge very positively to give braking power.

The stem skier should shorten his turn on steep slopes. The shorter the turn, the slower the speed at the end of the turn. A long stem on the steep equals high speed.

The stem skier can shorten his turn in two ways: first, make the move onto the stemmed ski a fast one.

The weight should be jumped onto the stemmed ski in one swift move. Springing onto the stemmed ski solidly as he stems it, the skier will push the ski into the turn. The turn will start fast, cross the fall line quickly, and be into a medium-steep traverse before the skier has picked up much speed.

Once the ski is well started, the skier *must* keep the weight on that ski. A lot of skiers who *think* they have their weight out there don't. They soon lean in toward the hill and fall.

The skier who has enough weight on the outside ski should be able to pick the inside ski *completely* off the snow at the end of the turn. He should try this as a "stem-improvement exercise," picking the inside ski up toward the end of the turn and holding it up. He will see that the extra weight he gets on the outside ski shortens the turn.

The other secret of good stem skiing on steeper slopes is to connect the turns.

The best way to connect the turns is to cut each turn short, so that the skier doesn't go all the way to a horizontal traverse before starting the next turn. If he is in a medium-steep traverse, he has gravity working for him. Gravity is a great help in starting a turn. Granted, the skier won't slow down quite so much at the end of each turn as he would if he went to a shallow traverse; yet it is tactically better to make three or four connected turns at medium speed than to make one turn to a shallow traverse, stop, and then painfully start up again. Starting a turn from a horizontal traverse is hard.

It is best to try to cut each turn short and start the next one early. If the turn becomes stuck, the skier should keep his skis in a medium-traverse angle by sideslipping, and start the next turn from this angle.

Above all, the stem skier should stay off continuously steep slopes. It is better to get to parallel by learning on moderate slopes. *Then* one can go to the steeper stuff.

PARALLEL ON STEEP SLOPES

A parallel skier on steep slopes shouldn't try to jump the skis around. The skier who jumps his skis is not solving the problem. The jump turn is too exhausting and acrobatic. The right way is to pull the skis up under you, turn them a few degrees, and come down again so the full weight is on the skis through the fall line. Jump-turning the skis through the fall line makes for a hard landing and a loss of balance.

The very best skiers keep their skis in the snow as much as possible, even during the unweighting. They flatten the skis to connect turns rather than unweighting completely, letting the skis brush through the snow, shoving them through the snow to the side for the start of the turn. This gives a smoother start.

The skis have to be nearly flat as the skier comes down on his skis again and pushes them sideways into the sliding part of the turn. If the skis are too much on edge as the skier brings his weight onto the skis again, they will "track" instead of turning. This means that the turn will stop right there, with the skier headed straight down the fall line—exactly what he is trying to prevent.

It helps if the skier lands softly, with plenty of knee action as he lands. This will keep the skis from being pushed too far into the snow, which might prevent their turning.

The problem of the landing, however, is not so prevalent as the problem of the take-off. Nine times out of ten, when the skis refuse to go through with a parallel turn on a slope, steep or not, the skier hasn't unweighted *enough*.

The lack of proper unweighting makes the skis balk in the transition between turns because there is still too much friction under them for the skier's body motion to break them into the turn. If the skier finds his skis refusing the turn, he should start exaggerating his "up." The problem will usually stop right away.

EXTRAORDINARY WEAPONS

The parallel skier has several extraordinary weapons when it comes to turning on a steep slope.

The first is the check. The purpose of the American system "parallel with check" is to teach this little trick. A good hard check before each turn will work wonders on a steep slope. The skier thrusts hard, checking his speed, and makes a good solid "platform" from which to take off for the unweighting and reverse into the next turn.

If the check and unweighting are timed right, he receives an assist from the "rebound" of the ski. The ski bends in a bow during the check and springs back. If the skier springs with it, he gets a boost. Springing with the ski saves a lot of work, so the expert skier prefers a good stiff ski for hard-snow conditions.

It is, of course, highly desirable to make short parallel turns to control speed in steep terrain. The shorter the turn the more it brakes speed.

SHORTENING THE PARALLEL TURN

The parallel skier shortens his turn in several ways. Basically, he wedels. He applies explosive reverse action to power the skis as far around as he can before letting the S and G forces take over. He should think of turning the skis rather than the shoulders; the shoulders take care of themselves.

A second way is to practice a little split rotation on the steep slope (Picture 254). This will set up a position for a powerful reverse to continue the turn. But, split rotation should not be overdone. About six inches of movement of the outside shoulder in the direction of the turn as the skier starts to come up for the unweighting is enough. The blocking of the shoulder movement should occur as the skier becomes weightless. Then, of course, the skier starts to reverse good and hard, and the skis keep turning

in the direction in which they were started.

The weight goes on the outside ski *early* in the turn. The skier does not wait for the ski to reach the fall line; he puts his weight on it almost immediately by proper use of the pole (Picture 255). The faster he puts his weight on the up-hill ski, the sooner it starts to act as a braking force. The ski, while it is unweighted, does not act as a braking force at all. "Weight on the up-hill ski" may sound contrary, but it is merely a case of weight on the outside ski of the coming turn, which is standard practice. By getting onto that ski *early*, the skier keeps the unweighting period very short and lengthens the braking period.

The turn itself also has to be short. Rather than hopping high, the skier down-unweights. The skier thrusts the skis to one side as he drops, letting the skis turn as he drops. He thrusts them out to the other side. The skis stay in the snow. The skier's body doesn't rise. There is always *some* pressure on the skis as they brush the snow. This procedure provides a much harder-braking series of turns than the normal up-motion wedel.

Cutting each turn off creates steep-slope parallel wedel. Too many skiers work hard at finishing each turn, edging around to a shallow traverse each time. They could be going down the hill with half the work if they cut the turns off short, putting in more turns per foot of descent.

CONNECTING TURNS

The skier should always plan to make his last turn so that he ends up facing the middle of the trail. Many skiers, unfortunately, make a turn, go into a traverse, and then come to a dead stop at the edge of the trail, facing the woods. It is much better for a skier to make a last turn *away* from the edge and *then* stop, so that he faces the middle. Then he is in a good position to start his next turn from a standstill; he has the whole width of the trail in front of him. The skier who always stops facing the

254. *Skier coming down Exhibition Run in Sun Valley is using split rotation to start his turn. Note the forward sweep of the left arm as he starts to unweight.*

255. *Junior Bounous getting his weight onto the uphill ski preparatory to making a downhill turn.*

middle of the trail may find that there don't *have* to be any last turns. Instead of stopping, he can go on making turns.

But suppose you *have* skied yourself into a corner. You are at a standstill facing the woods. This is where the "standing turns" come in. Basically, there are two turns that can be done at a standstill, enabling you to turn around and face the trail again. One is the kick turn, an exquisite maneuver. The more common one for beginners is the gambit of "walking the ski tails uphill." Both turns should be practiced on the flat of course.

WALKING TAILS UPHILL

To walk the tails uphill, the skier firmly plants both poles below him in the snow. The skis are in a horizontal position, well edged to keep the skier from sideslipping. The poles should be planted far enough away so that the skier can lean on them, straighten both elbows, and put his full weight on the poles. Poles should be about three or four feet apart on the snow.

First, the skier moves the tail of the uphill ski two feet or so farther up the hill, leaving the tip where it is. This puts him into a stem position. Then he moves the lower ski up, parallel with the upper ski. He is now facing somewhat down the hill, leaning his weight hard on the poles. This sounds like a tall order, but if the skier locks his elbows by keeping his arms straight, he will be able to do it nicely. He now keeps on stepping the skis around in a half circle until he is facing into the trail. At the very worst, if he should let go, he is on his way down the hill and can make a turn to face the middle of the trail.

THE KICK TURN

The kick turn is used on slopes too steep for the above. The skier puts poles ahead of him and leans forward on them, putting all the weight on the upper ski, which has to be edged well into the hill (Picture 256). Then he kicks the tip of the downhill ski into the air, sets the tail of that ski into the snow by his other ski tip, and lets the ski fall over into the opposite track (Picture 257). The skier now has one ski facing in each direction (Picture 258). The trick is to stay relaxed and take one's time. Once the first ski is down, the skier can lean forward onto that ski (Picture 259) and then, picking up the remaining ski, swing it around parallel to the first so that both skis now face into the trail (Picture 260).

The kick turn used to be taught to skiers on the first day or so on the slope, but wisdom has prevailed and it is now taught later, when the skier is more relaxed about his situation. The relaxation of the leg muscles is the key.

A third alternative, when the skier is standing face to face with unskiable terrain, is to start a vertical sideslip, then move the weight forward to force the tips to drop first and simultaneously stem the uphill ski. This will turn the skier out of the predicament. This "sideslip and stem" can be accomplished in a rather confined space. Three or four feet of clearance between the skier and the "edge" is enough. If he doesn't have the clearance, he can always back up until he does.

Best of all, one shouldn't get into this situation in the first place.

MOGUL PROBLEMS

The mogul is a modern phenomenon, brought about by the fact that skiers make fairly short turns on steep slopes. A mogul is a man-made mound; it grows because skiers tend to follow in each other's tracks down the hill. The snow gets pushed into a pile in the center of the turns. Other skiers, in going over the piles, pack them into polished little mounds—or big mounds if the slope is steep enough.

Moguls cost ski areas a lot of money. Ski area managers use men and machines to break moguls up and smooth them off, hoping to please the skiers. The skiers build up the moguls again.

One way out of this vicious circle is to persuade skiers to like moguls. Actually, moguls can be a lot of fun.

There are two ways of skiing them: slow and steady, over the tops, for one. Fast and sneaky around the bottoms is the other.

If one is a stem skier, one should try the high road. It helps if a mogul is nicely rounded on top, and many of them are. Then the skier approaches the mogul and skis up onto it. He stems as he reaches the top, and turns over the brim of the mogul, sideslipping the downhill face of it. Turning over a bump this way is easy. The tip and tail of the ski are out of the snow so the ski turns without much effort.

Once the skier comes off a mogul, sideslipping safely and slowly down the far face of it, he must now turn again on the next mogul, if possible. The art is to turn on almost every mogul to keep one's speed low.

256. *Start of kick turn in place.*

THE ART OF RIVER RUNNING

The low road is a more sophisticated mogul method and more beloved by the better skier.

He makes a short check turn up the side of the mogul and makes a hard check turn around the bottom and goes on. It is a real chess game. A highly skilled practitioner of the low-road method is called a "river runner" and his action, "river-running." In effect, the skier is running through the "rivers" between the moguls and avoiding the tops.

The skier who can do this at a good speed is in line for his expert skier's merit badge. The skier has to adjust his turns to the radius of the moguls. This means hitting the side at the right place, putting just enough edge in so that the ski carves around the mogul, coming to a heel-thrust check below the mogul very quickly

257. *Swinging first ski in kick turn.*

258. *Placing first ski in kick turn.*

so that he kills his speed before carving into the side of the next one. If he should make his second turn too short, the tails of his skis will swing against the neighbor mogul and that will throw him off balance.

The skier fits his rhythm to the rhythm of the moguls and it can be a great waltz.

Moguls often *do* have a rhythm to them, since they were originally formed by the turns of skiers. Sometimes you get an out-of-rhythm mogul, and then you have to go straight over it.

TAKING MOGULS STRAIGHT

The problem of going straight over a mogul is like the problem of handling any bump. The proper way is for the skier to "pull up" or lift his skis as he crosses the mogul. He then presses his skis down on the far side of the mogul;

then sets them quickly into a turn; he has by now presumably gained considerable headway. A few feet of straight running on a steep hill translates into speed almost as fast as that of a man in a free fall.

The skier hardly rises at all as he passes over the mogul. His legs draw up neatly under him and then press down again as he feels the mogul dropping away on the far side. "Lift and press" is the safe sequence.

The hard way to go over a mogul is to ride over it stiff-legged. This causes the mogul to lift the skier into the air. The aerial leap can be spectacular, of course, if the skier can handle the speed that this creates.

Any sudden dip in the slope can be handled by the same technique. The skier treats the far side of the dip as the face of a bump and lifts his skis out of the dip, departing unscathed.

Lastly, this technique can be used to handle a real drop-off. The skier tries to keep his skis

259. *Swinging second ski in kick turn.*

260. *Placing second ski in kick turn.*

on the snow rather than go sailing off the top of the drop. He simply pulls his skis up just before he gets to the lip of the drop. (The name of the maneuver is "pre-jump.") The skier is then dropping as he goes over the lip. As he passes the lip, he presses his skis into the snow, hard, and maintains contact with it as it drops away under him. As long as he is in contact with the snow, he can make turns and control himself.

261. *Pepi Gramshammer, a world champion, formerly from Austria and now at Vail, does a pre-jump over a lip. He is shown extending his legs to touch down again at the end of the pre-jump. The maneuver meant that he avoided being tossed in the air over the lip of the drop-off in the background.*

Chapter 11

EASTERN AND WESTERN SKI TECHNIQUES

The inside story on ice—too little snow; the other extreme—too much snow

A friend of mine who had moved to the West once skied Aspen with me. As we finished off a trail, his skis struck ice with a nasty sound. He turned around and said, "What was that? We never hear that sound out here!"

Ice is mainly an eastern problem. The advice below is dedicated to the two thirds of the ski population that lives in the East.

There is only one solution to real "blue ice." That is to keep a pair of "blue-ice skis." A ski school head I know keeps a pair of skis that he takes out only four or five times a year, when the slopes go to sheet ice. (This is what is meant by blue ice.) At the end of the year, he trades them for a new pair. The edges of his blue-ice skis never see much use, and so, when they are used, they cut into the ice like knives. There is nothing like new edges for ice.

The second-best thing is to re-sharpen the edges on Old Faithfuls, your only pair of skis. However, re-sharpened edges don't cut quite like new ones. But a sharp edge *is* the single, best anti-ice device. The sides of an edge should form a square, not a round corner.

Fortunately, most ice on the slopes is not pure and blue; it is white ice. The best thing a skier can do with a white-ice patch is to run straight over it without making turns. He should make his turn on the far side. He must not be proud: he should put about six inches between the skis for stability, run over the ice parallel, and bend both knees just slightly inward to turn the skis up on their inside edges. This keeps the skis from "wandering" over the ice as the skier runs across it.

Incidentally, sometimes when a skier has trouble with skis-wandering during a straight run, ice or not, he can straighten them out by putting them very slightly on the inside edges. If his skis wander all the time, they are warped or worn out or too soft.

SIDESLIPPING AND TURNING ON ICE

If the skier doesn't want to build up the extra speed, it is perfectly possible to sideslip ice rather than schuss it. The skier has to "go" with the lower ski, with no hesitation. The sideslip will be a fast one. He must not try to make a stop check in the middle of the patch or he'll lose everything. Sideways speed may seem fast, but it really is not. It is just a question of getting used to the idea of sideways speed. The skier keeps the skis fairly flat and stands relaxed, very straight, and balanced over them;

he will arrive at the other side of the patch with as good control as he could expect, given the size of the ice patch.

The skier *can* make turns on ice. He uses very little edging. The skier who edges hard on ice is going to get "chatter" in his skis. These are very unsettling rapid vibrations that make the skis hard to control. Hard edging may also cause the skis to "track" rather than turn. But the skier exaggerates the comma from the waist. Getting *more weight* on the outside ski is a lifesaver here.

BOILER-PLATE PROBLEMS

A more common condition is near-ice, or "boiler plate," a condition that often persists on a whole mountain. If the skier has good edges, he can turn fairly well on moderate boiler-plate slopes. But, again, he has to under-edge and not try to make too many hard turns. Nice, easy rounded turns and *plenty of weight* on the outside ski are called for. If he gets into difficulties, he should sideslip rather than stop, at least for the first few feet. If he *has* to stop fast, he can do it, but he has to make a very muscular and exaggerated comma that almost bends him double. Most skiers don't have too many stops like that in them on a given day.

Boiler-plate turns are ones where I sometimes like to forget parallel and use stem christies, just for the sake of keeping my edges into harder contact with the slope at all times.

There usually are alleviating circumstances with boiler plate. The first is that the ski area manager may take pity and send up a few snow tractors to break up the boiler plate on the intermediate slopes. In this case, one should ski those. Or there may be trails that face south on the slope. If this is so, and there is a bit of sun, these trails will be considerably more hospitable, for they soften slightly. If one trail is much more heavily used than the others, this slope will be cut up enough after a while to become passable skiing for all.

SKI THE SIDES

Often, when the middle of the trail is hard, the sides have loose easy snow. The skier pilots from one side to the other, making his turn on whatever loose snow he finds. This may sound simple, but there is great art to it. Nothing is so stirring (to an eastern skier) as seeing a real pro go down a slope of boiler plate touching bits of loose snow here and there, skiing as smoothly as if he were in ankle-deep powder. A skier who can spot loose snow patches and string them together in a series of turns is a fine slope strategist.

Some of the time, the sides of the trails are simply swimming with snow. The skier cuts his turns short and keeps connecting them on one side of the trail. He stays right in the ribbon of snow.

Even a stem skier can do this. Unfortunately, most stem skiers don't. They know how to make the full stem turn from shallow traverse to shallow traverse, and that is all they know. They ski out in the middle, fighting boiler plate like a Class D farm-team rookie swinging at curves.

I would venture to say that a stem skier, using wide-track quick stems, *could* stay along the sides using short connected turns.

Boots have an effect on skiing boiler plate. A boot with a good stiff "upper" will make skiing icy trails very much easier than a soft boot with worn-out leather around the ankles. And when icy conditions prevail, this is the time for the skier to lace or buckle the boot as tight as he can and still maintain circulation in his feet.

DEEP SNOW CHALLENGES: POWDER

This brings us to the question of "surplus snow."

The first kind of surplus-snow condition is the best: powder. Some eastern areas boast that they have "heavy powder" on a given day, but what they have is *not* powder. It is just new wet snow. Powder is light, airy, and *dry* by definition.

Powder is delightful. A covering of two inches over hard-packed snow turns average skiing into great skiing. Four inches is heaven. But after that, the skier has to vary his technique a bit. By the time there is a foot of powder, skiing is almost another sport altogether.

The skier going through a foot of new powder will have sensations unlike anything on hard-pack. In the first place, the powder will tend to snatch his inside ski away, cause it to "hook" to the inside. In the second place, it makes the turn down the hill very much harder, and the turn up the hill somewhat easier. Skiers not used to powder find themselves continually running out to the side in a shallow traverse,

262. *The square stance of the powder skier is illustrated here by the skier doing a traverse in powder at Sun Valley. The "square" stance with shoulders at right angles to the skis is more like the Canadian style of skiing, or the French. Both tend to have a squarer traverse than the Austrian or American styles.*

unable to make a decent turn back down the hill again.

The western skiers have worked out a whole technique for handling powder which is quite different from the way eastern skiers ski. In the first place, the Westerner skis much squarer over the skis (Picture 262). There is very little reversing or angulation. The western skier makes a short rotation to start a split rotation turn and then rides a long carved arc with the *whole* body leaning inward in a diagonal direction (Picture 263). Long before they reach the traverse line, they bounce up quite high, rotate slightly, lean inward to the other side, and ride out a new turn. The whole thing looks exasperatingly easy. But it is an entire technique in itself.

The principles underlying the western style are as follows.

In the first place, the skis must be pretty evenly weighted in deep powder. The reason that the Easterner finds his inside ski being snatched away is that the snow grabs the ski that has less weight on it and tends to twist it away. The legs have to be actively *squeezed* together in the parallel turn, to keep the snow from piling in between the legs and splitting the skis.

Angulation tends to put the weight on the outside ski, and this disrupts the even weighting. A "square," upright style weights the skis evenly.

A little rotation seems to work better in starting the turn, because it pulls the tips gently into the turn, allowing the skier to keep his square stance with less disturbance—and the square stance is the key to the style (Picture 265).

The western skier uses just a little bit of reverse toward the end of the turn—but not enough to endanger the delicate balance. It is for this reason that the western skiers have been advocates of split rotation: it works so well in powder.

Finally, the high bounce, which gets the skis partly out of the snow, also allows the skier to "change edges" by leaning to the other side. In effect, the western-style skier edges by using

263. *The powder skier typically edges by leaning the whole body toward the inside of the turn, as Nick Fiore is doing here at Badger Pass. The standard reverse skier would be in a comma here, "looking downhill."*

264. *The danger of leaning toward the center of the turn with the whole body is aptly illustrated here; the skier can recover less easily if he leans too far in than if he used the comma. However, the inward lean of the whole body makes it easier to weight both skis evenly than when in the comma.*

265. *The western style: both skiers here are just coming down from their unweighting and are turning toward each other in split rotation, which gives them a square stance.*

his whole body, setting the skis on edge by "leaning in."

The western skier also sits back somewhat, but not much. He is wearing his powder skis—with soft tips. Those tend to surface rather than dive. As long as the tips tend to surface, the skier is in no trouble. If the tips dive, of course, he is.

Lastly, the western skier doesn't wait for the skis to come around to a shallow traverse. He cuts the turn short so that he never gets into a shallow traverse, making a series of long, sweeping christies *along* the fall line, rather than full parallel turns. This keeps his speed up and prevents the skis from going off across the hill in a shallow traverse.

What can the eastern skier do if he is caught in powder with his stiff skis?

He has to follow western principles as well as he can. He sits back on the skis. He unweights more, uses split rotation and a very gentle reverse at the end; he must cut his turns off so that he skis along the fall line all the time; he has to adopt a square stance to keep the weight even on the skis, and squeeze his legs together to keep them from being split.

266. *The skier here forgot to keep his legs squeezed together. The powder is grabbing his right ski and is about to twist it away from the skier.*

267. *It is possible to use the reverse stance in powder. This skier at Aspen is less reversed than the ordinary non-powder skier would be at this point, but he is nevertheless in a reverse.*

268. *These two skiers are making wedel turns in powder. Both are about to start turns to their left. The upper skier has already led off with his outside hand to start the split-rotation wedel, or submarine wedel, and the lower skier is about to do the same.*

Above all, he ought to maintain good speed. If he can hold his skis together and hold good speed, he has got the powder all but mastered. If he slows down, it starts to master him. This means sweeping turns, close to the fall line.

It *is* possible to wedel in deep powder; this is the so-called "submarine." It is a split-rotation wedel with very flat skis, and exaggerated reverses. The skier stays very low, and slithers his skis back and forth *under* the snow. The submarine wedel is a forced turn, and it is not easy to force a turn in deep snow. The "submarine" is a series of connected sideslips in powder. The skier *flattens* the skis and *pushes* them out to the side to make his turn, and he *down-unweights* to start each turn. Down-unweighting is the key to short turns in powder (Picture 268).

STEMMING THE POWDER

What of the stem skier in powder?

His best bet is a "step-stem." This means that he should *lunge* onto the ski as he stems it. (This is about the only way he can kick the ski into the stem position in deep powder.) He cuts the turn off fairly soon, so that he stays pretty much in the fall line. His speed will be kept down by the resistance of the snow, and so he won't really have to get into a shallow traverse.

He exaggerates his up-unweighting a bit, which makes the step-stem a sort of leaping stem. The expert version of this, the "dipsy doodle," was invented as a way of getting through powder by the first American racer to win international recognition, Dick Durrance. It is effective, but not aesthetic. The action is reminiscent of Eliza in *Uncle Tom's Cabin*, jumping from ice cake to ice cake ahead of the bloodhounds.

HEAVY DEEP SNOW

The next condition is wet, heavy new snow (in its worst form called "mashed potatoes"). It is a layer of deep snow of thick consistency lying on top of the base snow. An inch or so merely improves the skiing, but with three or four inches, new tactics are called for; six inches of the heavy stuff is something fierce.

The general answer for the parallel skier is to stay *near the fall line*, making "submarine" wedel turns across the fall line. The skier has to keep his skis flat and slicing through this stuff to master it.

As with powder, the heavy wet snow makes it hard to turn into the fall line. The skier who cuts his turns short is going to have a much easier time of things. He will constantly down-unweight to start the next turn into the fall line, without coming out of the snow in a big hop. It is better to keep the skis *in* the snow, even when the skis are down-unweighted, because the critical point of the wet-snow turn is the point where the skier comes down from his unweighting and puts his weight on the skis again. If he comes down too hard with too much edge, the ski will "track" and won't turn.

The skier who is caught in the shallow traverse, or who finds the snow too heavy to "move" at the start of the turn, may then *have* to resort to lifting the skis completely out of the snow to get them turning. In some cases, he will find himself so bogged down that the best way out is to use the two-pole turn. He puts both poles in the snow and comes out of the snow by pulling the skis up under him. He then turns the skis with reverse power and thrusts them down into the snow again, fairly flat and already turning. The use of two poles enables the skier to cut down the violence of his motions so that he has a smooth re-entry into the snow when he comes down on his skis again.

The skier who over-edges during his turn in this kind of snow will find his ski tracking straight down the hill. He is now in a very bad position to start the turn going again. In this case, his best bet is to "skate up." He completes the turn with a series of skating steps very much like the Foeger exercises described earlier.

269. *Wedeling in a small amount of powder calls for less of the split-rotation action, but the skis have to be broken into the turn very forcefully. The skiers here are using normal wedel to make their way through powder.*

270. *Powder can be deep: Sepp Froehlich of the Sun Valley ski school making waves through hip-deep powder in a typical powder-skier's square stance.*

STEMMING IN HEAVY SNOW

The stem skier can make his way fairly well through two or three inches of wet snow. For one thing, his speed will be braked by the heavy consistency of the snow. For another, the stem skier turns without any unweighting, so that the problem of re-entry is avoided. But he must not over-edge. The fairly flat ski will shear through heavy snow where the heavily edged ski will stick and start tracking.

When it comes to deeper wet snow, the stem skier has to stay near the fall line and connect the turns. If he gets stuck in a shallow traverse, his best bet is to stop completely and step his tails up the slope a little. Then he is facing downhill and can start off a new turn series.

One final note about deep powder and heavy wet snow: while ice and boiler plate may be awful stuff, they make safe going (very few skiers suffer injuries in the course of negotiating boiler plate; the skis will slide over in a fall). Not so in heavy wet snow or deep powder. The skis will tend to lodge in the snow and exert leverage on the skier's legs when he falls. Every ski patrolman expects heavy soft stuff to keep him two to three times as busy as on a day when the snow is hard.

It is of utmost importance, therefore, to the skier that he check his release bindings on a day when he is going into deep powder or loose new snow. (We shall discuss bindings in detail in Chapter 12.)

To summarize: first, connect the turns. Second, use down-unweighting in the fall line. Third, keep the skis flat in the snow if possible, that is, don't over-edge. Fourth, use double-pole turns if you get caught and can't start the turn. Fifth, step-turn out if you have trouble finishing the turn. Last, make sure your bindings are adjusted.

Chapter 12

EQUIPMENT I

What to do about spending money for gear

The question of money is paramount when the skier thinks of equipment. Good equipment costs money and bad equipment costs pleasure.

Possibly the simplest solution at first is to rent skis, poles, and boots at a rental shop near home or at the ski area. The new skier may decide against the sport after a try, in which case his investment is minimal. But there are pitfalls. The rental shop may be good or it may be bad. Many of them are bad.

A shop near home knows that the skier is a local person and consequently might serve his needs better than a shop at a ski area. (To be sure, there *are* plenty of good rental shops at ski areas.) The second advantage in renting from a store nearby is that the skier can go in during the week, get fitted, get the binding setting checked (most important), and get the financial dealings over with—all before he reaches the ski area. This saves him up to two hours of skiing time.

The critical feature of rental equipment is the release binding. Most rental places, unfortunately, use cheap release bindings, which are like cheap insurance: they don't protect you where you need protection most.

Second, the rental boot is usually fairly soft and doesn't fit well. Or, more recently, the shops have stiff plastic boots that are extremely uncomfortable unless they fit exactly.

One way out of the dilemma is to rent a pair of short skis, preferably three-footers. The three-footer doesn't really need a safety binding, and the stiffness and fit of the boot are not nearly so important. The skier is introduced to the sport without having to manipulate six- and seven-foot boards on his feet.

Note: the four-foot ski should have a release binding, although this is not critical, and the five-footer *definitely* should have release bindings.

For about the same money as it might cost to rent a three-footer for a couple of weekends, the skier can *buy* wood three-footers with simple bindings ($12 to $20). He doesn't need to rent poles at all, and so he saves there as well.

It must be noted, in all fairness, that there are not likely to be more than a small minority of skiers at any area wearing three-footers. If a skier is worried about appearances, it may be that he would rather struggle with the full-length ski. The middle way is to rent a pair of five-footers or buy a pair ($25 and up for wood, about $100 for metal).

Let us assume now that the skier has decided to go skiing at least ten weekends, often enough to justify an investment in equipment. Figuring that minimum expense for a ski weekend will come to $30 a day, exclusive of equipment, his investment in the sport will be $600 for those ten weekends. More likely, it will be nearer $800. In light of these considerations, the expense of equipment assumes its proper proportions. If the skier has to worry excessively about investing in equipment, he may not be able to afford to ski regularly. He *can* afford it, via a weekend or two on rental equipment, however.

BUYING BINDINGS

Back to our new serious skier. The first item he should consider is the least glamorous, the bindings. More than 95 per cent of the bindings today are release bindings. A well-designed release binding will keep the skier out of trouble.

Trouble comes when the ski twists or bends the ankle. With a release binding working properly, the binding will let go of the boot before the skier feels too much of a twist.

On a given day, two skiers out of a thousand will have some injury that requires medical attention. This figure could be cut in half, or better, if release bindings were all properly designed and maintained. Two out of a thousand is not a high figure, but over ten weekends it adds up to 2 per cent of skiers skiing ten weekends. Release bindings are necessary. Of the people who have been hurt, almost 100 per cent were skiing out of control or had bad release bindings or both.

When you buy bindings, ignore all that don't have a release at *both* the toe and the heel. Both are needed. The heel release is usually designed to let go in a forward fall, and the toe in a sideways fall, although with some bindings both releases are designed to let go in all kinds of falls.

The "unit" bindings, costing $25 and up, come with toe and heel together, as a unit. Of these, Cubco and Miller are the best known. Both require boot plates, or metal plates on the boot heel and toe. Both should be shop-mounted, even if you are a good shopman yourself.

The new Gertsch binding is a unit binding with a removable boot plate and is considered one of the best of the current leading binding designs.

The other kinds of bindings are sold as separate heel and toe releases.

The new "step-in" heel binding does away

with the long spring cable which had to be threaded through cable leads along the sides of the skis. The cables sometimes stuck in these leads and would not release. Avoid cable heel bindings.

The other new heel release is the "short cable," which is not dangerous and not expensive. (Marker Telemat is one example.)

An outstanding toe release at present is the Look Nevada. It gives way under continuous pressure and yet holds you on the ski during short, sharp twists in which you want the ski to stay on. Another interesting new release is the Spademan, with a small central boot plate; it works very well.

Bindings ordinarily should be mounted by a

271. *The Gertsch binding is a new step-in type that comes as a unit heel and toe release. Boot plate is removable from boot and does away with poor release due to swelling and shrinking of the boot.*

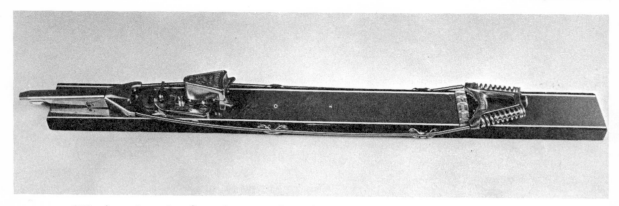

272. *A section of a ski with a toe release (Marker) on the front of the ski, and cable heel release (Marker) on the back. This is called the front-throw heel release, because the release is actually made by the lever mechanism at the very front of the section, to the left; this lever is called the front-throw. Cables run back through the side hitches on the side of the ski to the heel-spring farthest to the right.*

ski shop, unless you know what you are doing. But the shop itself should have a good reputation with the binding-maker. There are shops that mount some bindings properly, others improperly. The safest way is to write to the binding manufacturer, once you have picked the binding, and ask them to recommend a shop in your area. It is worth a trip to get bindings mounted the way they should be. Otherwise you may be taking a lot of the release potential out of the binding.

CHECKING YOUR BINDING

There are a few very practical things you can check to make sure the binding behaves up to its potential.

(1) Make sure that the top of the toe piece doesn't squeeze down on the boot tip. Your boot should be held in the binding by the forward pressure exerted by the heel binding, not by excessive downward pressure at the toe piece. Too much downward pressure on the boot at the toe may cause a binding to stick. If the boot is being squeezed, you will find an adjustment—if the binding is of a reputable make—enabling you to raise the toe piece. The toe piece should touch the top of the boot toe but not squeeze it down.

(2) Once the boots are fitted to the binding in the shop, keep the left boot in the left binding and the right boot in the right binding. Don't switch skis from foot to foot unless you readjust the bindings. Boots might be slightly different in length. (Mark one ski in some way to distinguish it.)

(3) Make sure that, if you have your boot notched to fit the binding, that the notches are of equal depth. Unequal notch depths will cause the boot to release more easily in one direction than the other, and you can never get the binding at its best setting.

(4) Make sure that the boot is centered in the binding when you ski. If the boot is off center, it will release hard to one side.

(5) Don't let the nailheads or screwheads protrude from the ski or from the soles of the boots. They will block the release mechanism.

(6) If you are using a cable, keep it at a low tension, so that it doesn't "mash" the boot against the toe piece in front. Too much pressure against the toe piece will raise the release threshold of the binding. With too little pressure, of course, the boot won't stay in.

(7) If you have a long cable, the rear side

hitches or leads should not be more than two thirds of the way back along the boot. If they are farther back than that, they may "kink" the cable and foil release.

(8) Use a leather strap or thong to keep the ski from running off if it releases (this is a very good thing to have—you may lose the ski, and a runaway ski is highly dangerous). Attach it to the cable back of the rear side hitches, not in front, otherwise you may foul up the cable release.

(9) Lubricate the working parts of your release bindings with graphite or silicone spray to make sure they don't stick.

(10) Check the settings of the release bindings frequently.

A little more detail on this last point: there is a way to check the toe release, roughly. That is to buckle the boot onto one ski and then try to push the empty boot toe out with the thumbs of both hands. This test should determine whether you have sufficient pressure to keep you in if you are an intermediate skier. If you are a hard skier and need more pressure to hold you in, you can set your toe pieces to release less readily.

There is a much more scientific way of doing this. Buy a $15-gadget called "Release Check," made by a designer named Gordon Lipe. The gadget will give you a reading on your toe release that will be much more accurate and will check the release on both sides. Release Check will teach you a lot about safety and safety bindings.

As for checking the heel release, the proper way is to put one ski on and then simply try to pull your heel out of the release by force, pulling slowly forward. You should be able to pull your heel out without resorting to a forward lunge for an intermediate-skier setting.

If you are an expert skier, you will probably want to tighten the heel release more than indicated in the test above. This eliminates some of the release potential at the low end of the scale. You won't release in a slow-twist fall, during which the ski slowly twists around. On the other hand, the ski will stay on if you want to make twenty-foot jumps and come down hard. You have to make a choice.

For the beginning and intermediate skier, it is definitely better to stay on the loose side, at least in the beginning. The slow-twist fall is rare for the expert but frequent for the beginner.

I have dwelt on bindings at length, because of their importance and because badly designed bindings and badly set bindings hold skiing back. Not many beginners come back to the sport after an injury. Gordon Lipe has tested various brands of release bindings and has found that most best-selling brands are pretty good releases, and that there are dozens of cheap off-brand release bindings that are no good at all.

If someone tells you that boots are the most important item a skier buys, don't believe it. A poor boot won't sprain your ankle.

BUYING BOOTS

In terms of pure comfort, the boot is *the* prime factor. It is also the most important factor in edge control and in governing the direction of the ski. The skier's foot performs hundreds of little reflex actions every minute to keep the ski running in the direction the skier wants to point it. If you doubt this, take a pair of cheap rubber ski boots—such as are made in Japan and sell for about $6—and try them. You will find that the ski won't go where you point it. The reason is that the boot doesn't adequately transmit the reflex actions of the foot to the ski.

The *most* important function of the boot is steering, not edging. The boot should fit very closely over the whole lower foot, particularly at the ball of the foot. Stiffness of the ankle of the boot, while helpful in edging, is not so important as the close fit at the narrow part of the foot where the steering is done.

Fit is important to comfort. If your boot hurts, you won't want to ski. Your feet are very delicately constructed, but they carry great pressures. Overload one area of the foot and the pain becomes excruciating. If bad fit ends in a blister or "bone bruise," your skiing is over for a while.

There is hardly a boot worth wearing that costs less than $40, and you probably ought to spend $60 at a minimum. The boots form the connection between the skis and the body and they should take most of the strain of the job off the feet. The boot has to be rugged, and rugged materials are expensive. So is good workmanship.

BUCKLE BOOTS

Buckle boots are the thing. They have the great advantage that you can buckle them down in cold weather and unbuckle them on the lift to let the blood circulate and warm the feet. This enables you to keep your boots good and tight in cold weather, which is hard to do with lace boots.

Also, the buckle boot can be tightened up in seconds when the boot warms and stretches from the heat of the foot, as happens with any leather. This means you don't have to take time out to relace. In an old-fashioned lace boot, relacing took ten to fifteen minutes, several times a day.

When buying boots, take your time. Visit at least three stores and try on various brands. Each brand is made over a different "last." One boot may not be "right" for your foot, another may be. Some lasts have a high instep, others a low instep. The instep is particularly critical because you want to be able to put pressure on top of the instep, just behind the ball of the foot, to make sure that the boot is tight at that point; otherwise steering is lost. But, if you put pressure on the top of the instep and the boot does not fit under the instep, you will have an uncomfortable boot.

The second critical point is at the heel. The

273. *The Henke plastic boot. Almost all boots today are made of artificial materials which last longer than leather.*

boot should be tight enough so that the heel cannot be readily raised off the sole of the boot, even if someone holds the boot heel and you try to pull the heel of your foot upward. However, this is not quite so critical as the first point. If you have a boot that is very snug and tight over the top of the instep and around the ball of the boot, you can accept a little "give" at the heel.

If you have a long, narrow foot, you may be better off getting a made-to-order boot. But sending your foot measurements to a bootmaker (they are nearly all in Europe) is no guarantee of a fit. These made-to-orders frequently come back fitting badly. The only sure way is to have it done while you are in Europe so that the fit can be checked. You can also send a plaster cast of your foot. Any good orthopedic foot doctor and some orthopedic stores will make you a cast.

When you are trying on boots, wear one thin sock and one thick one on each foot. This is the best combination for the slopes, and you should wear it when being fitted.

The skier must bend forward at the ankle when he skis, to down-unweight and to execute other moves. There is no sense, then, in getting a boot that is too high in front. It will cut into the shin bone when you bend forward. This is particularly true of stem skiers whose ankles are bent forward a good deal of the time. In fact, most stem skiers are better off with the top buckle of most boots undone.

Unless you are a hard skier, do not buy a hard boot. Buy a medium boot. Only those skiers who ski a great deal of the time can afford the luxury of a very stiff boot. You have to get used to it gradually, shifting to older and more comfortable boots to give your feet a rest.

Today there are all-Fiberglas boots, all-synthetic leather boots, and combination plastic-leather boots. The advantage of plastic is that it does not stretch or break down with age. Yet, all plastic boots must be fitted with *greater care* than ever, since they (1) are buckle boots and (2) will not change shape at all to fit the foot, as leather will.

Chapter 13

EQUIPMENT II

Skis, poles, and clothes and how they relate to skiing

There are really two main choices when it comes to skis. First, length: short or long? Second, material: wood, metal, or Fiberglas?

We have debated the question of length sufficiently. The question of material is a matter of cost. A set of wood skis will perform fairly well provided you are willing to pay over $40 for them. But they have a tendency to warp, which means that your skiing will get lopsided: you turn more easily in one direction than in the other. And they lose their "life" or resilience very soon.

Metal skis, which begin somewhere around $100 (for the cheap ones), will not warp or wear out nearly so soon. Also, metal skis can be designed to turn more readily than the wood. Beginner's metal skis are designed just that way. The Head beginner and Hart beginner are outstandingly easy to turn. Each brand has its own partisans. (Probably the best buy in metal skis is the Hart off-brand known as Mercury. It is the same ski as the Hart beginner, but about $20 cheaper.)

The more expensive Heads and Harts go to about $180 for Head racing skis, and $200 for the Hart Javelin, a prestige ski. The beginner's models, although they turn well and easily, do not track so well as the more expensive "expert" models. On the other hand, the expert models are harder to turn. You can't have it both ways. A beginning skier is much better off with the beginner's models.

FIBERGLAS SKIS

The Fiberglas ski is constructed of anything from 100-per cent Fiberglas to a 10-per cent Fiberglas covering on wood skis. Good Fiberglas skis are being made, and the best are very smooth-skiing products, easy over the bumps and steady in tracking. But there hasn't been a shakedown in the field yet, and many new brands are untested. The longest-standing brand is Kneissl's series—White Star, Red Star, Blue Star, Magic 77. The White Star comes in about $215 and the others somewhat less. Yamaha is a leading economy Fiberglas ski ($90 or so). At present, however, Fiberglas skis are usually more expensive than metal and less durable; they do not keep their looks. (Fiberglas skis scuff up more easily.) The skier who buys today's Fiberglas is buying a ride, not durability.

It may be comforting, after all this, to know that there is a reasonably-priced piece of ski equipment: the pole. Excellent aluminum poles can be had for $12 to $15. There are lovely light aluminum-alloy poles at $25 to $35, but it takes an expert skier to appreciate them. The top "name" brand is Scott, who makes an aluminum-alloy pole with a very nice "pistol grip" that helps the skier to flick out his pole for the coming turn.

The main question regarding poles is height.

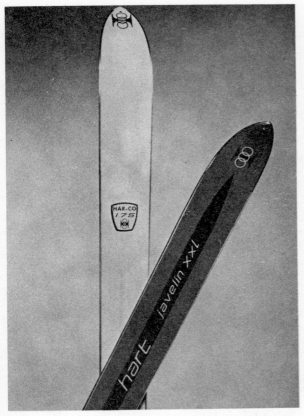

274. *A typical modern ski made by Hart Ski Company. It has layers of Fiberglas (E and H) and a wood core.*

I favor a long pole for the recreational skier. Stand the pole on the floor. The handle should come up hard against the underside of the arm, next to the body, when the skier stands normally. The expert skier uses a shorter pole for maneuverability, but the average skier uses the pole for support while standing and while unweighting. If the pole is too short, he'll have to lean over too far to use it. The skier also uses the pole to push himself along the flat and to climb. Here again, length is good.

The other pole consideration is the hand strap. The strap should be adjustable—and broad enough so that it won't cut into the hand when the skier leans on it.

The proper position for the hand inside the strap is one in which the skier grasps both strap and pole and lets the strap take the strain, rather than holding the pole handle in a death grip. The skier should be able to use the pole with the fingers unclasped if he is utilizing the strap to take the strain in the proper manner.

WARMTH AND SKIING

The sport of skiing is built up partly of a series of interdependent judgments on equipment and clothes. If the skier starts out with good, functional clothes, the rest of the sport becomes easier. If the skier has warm underclothes, for instance, he won't have to wear markedly heavy sweaters and parkas. He will be freer to move. Also, if the underclothes keep the central part of

275. *Howard Head, father of the metal ski. Head spent years working out his design for the ski before he made any money on it. He is now retired, but his idea marches on.*

twenty-five-mile-an-hour wind and still be comfortable. (Both BVD and Duofold make quilted underwear.)

The next warmest kind is net underwear, and after that, double-ply long underwear. Both are useful in temperatures from zero to twenty-five above. The ski instructor, who is at the area all week long, has time to become acclimated to the cold and probably does not need anything but net underwear. The recreational skier *does* need warmer underwear, unless he sleeps outdoors all week to get acclimated.

the body warm, the hands will be warm and the skier will move the poles better. And he will have warmer feet, which means they'll be more sensitive to the proper edge needed for the skis.

The eastern skier particularly needs warm underwear. Temperatures in the East often go below zero. If there is a wind, it is impossible to ski comfortably in below-zero weather without quilted underwear. This is rather bulky, soft, pliable stuff, and it doesn't hinder the skier's movements. It is built along the same principles as the quilted parka. A full suit of this underwear costs about $10 to $25 and can save a weekend. Quilted underwear makes it possible to ride a chair lift at fifteen below zero in a

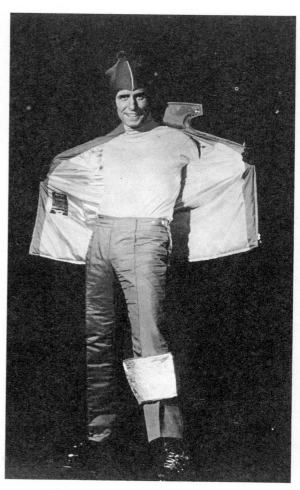

276. *Anba's new "thin skin" ensembles utilize a new space-age aluminized nylon, which serves to reflect body heat and keeps you warm without extra padding.*

277. *Spinnerin's over-the-boot pants and parka outfit.*

278. *Stretch pants. Some models come even tighter and more form fitting. Where else but in a circus or out skiing could you wear something like this? The answer used to be nowhere, but not any more. Housewives now go shopping in stretch pants.*

STRETCH PANTS

Stretch pants do make the wearer more attractive (in most cases), and because they are close to the skier's skin, they help him get the feel of the correct positions more easily. Stretch pants run from $30 to $75. The most crucial point about stretch pants is whether the stirrup, which goes under the foot, is broad enough to hold the pants down without cutting the skier's instep. It should be at least two inches wide at the narrowest point and should be made of stretch material like the pants themselves. Some pants are attached "over the boot" and do not go under the foot, a very sensible innovation.

The alternative to stretch pants is knickers. They are less expensive and more comfortable. If you are riding a long distance to the slope in ski clothes, they are *much* more comfortable. And they are as acceptable as stretch pants.

Levi's are acceptable, as well, particularly for those under twenty-five. The Levi's are open at the bottom, however, and you should expect your socks to get wet if the temperature is above freezing.

With proper underwear, the skier needs only a parka and a sweater under it. If you have a mountain parka, which is quite bulky and filled with eiderdown, you won't need more than a medium-weight sweater. Mountain parkas have

279. *Medium-weight quilted parka. About right for the Western slopes. For the East, a skier should get a more heavily quilted parka with more insulation to it.*

been coming on the market lately in response to a sensible demand for warmer clothes. Fashion people have in the past been imbued with the "thin look." The thin look is great when the sun's out and the temperature stands at twenty-five or so, but below that, it is forbiddingly cool to ski in a "thin look" outfit.

The mountain-type parka filled with down makes much more sense.

The cost of a mountain parka is somewhere around $56.

The standard, non-mountain parka is about half as warm and costs about half as much. On cold days it has to be supplemented by a good thick ski sweater underneath. The thinner, more fashionable "thin look" parka is also quilted or insulated, but it is not really warm enough, as I have said, for the run of eastern skiing, although it might fare better under the milder western conditions or in Europe. The East, by and large, has the coldest recreational alpine skiing conditions in the world.

All parkas ought to have a hood for riding the chair lift. No amount of warm clothing replaces the wind-breaking action of the hood on a parka.

Standard wear under the sweater is a turtle-neck T shirt, and standard headgear is a knitted hat or headband.

MITTENS AND GLOVES

The remaining item of importance is mittens or gloves.

Some wear mittens and some wear gloves. Gloves enable you to handle the poles better, and to work on the bindings without taking them off. But to wear gloves when the temperature is below twenty above, you have to be well acclimated. The average skier should have a pair of warm wool mittens under a good tough pair of mitten covers to ski in cold weather.

There are light mitten covers for warm weather, made of poplin, but they are good only down to about twenty degrees. Below that, you should have a pair of thick leather mitten covers. They will hold you down to about ten above.

After that, you need *insulated* mitten covers. The combination of the insulated mitten cover and wool under-mitten is a bit clumsy when it comes to handling the poles, but that is a lot better than being miserable. The wool under-mitten or liner can be bought almost anywhere for a dollar or so. The insulated leather mitten cover can be had (Weiss is a very good brand) for $8 to $10.

If the weather warms, you can always discard the under-mitten and go with the cover only. Or shift to a pair of gloves.

There *are* a couple of new glove types on the market that are bidding to make the idea that gloves are only for the warmer weather obsolete. First, there is the down glove, and then there is the Scott "Twenty Below" glove, which some of its users swear will keep you warm to twenty below. Lastly, there is an Astroglove, modeled after the astronaut's own, with aluminum foil in it, among other materials: glove technology seems on the rise these days.

GLASSES AND GOGGLES

Glasses and goggles are standard equipment for most skiers. The wind, flying flakes, too much sunlight, fog—all require some help for the eyes.

Even the best goggles and glasses fog easily (the only exception at the present is the Abercrombie & Fitch No-Fog), but most glasses and goggles can be rendered temporarily fog-free by one of the fog-preventive liquids or sprays. Try to get one from a local ski store; it's worth hunting around until you find one that works for you. Impaired vision makes skiing much less fun.

Except for extreme conditions, such as high speed (forty miles an hour) and strong wind, high-quality sunglasses are better than goggles. Ordinary optical-grade sunglasses give you much better peripheral vision than goggles will. They get fogged less easily and are more easily wiped clean of fog and sticky snowflakes. Only racers need goggles, ordinarily.

Don't buy cheap sunglasses. The plastic lens is

softer and scratches more easily than glass, but in a fall it won't shatter and so endanger your eyes. Better a few scratches on the lens of the glasses than on your face.

If you need prescription glasses to ski, have your prescription made up for plastic lenses. It's worth it as a safety measure.

Don't buy wrap-around glasses: they fog up more easily, are harder to clean, and distort your peripheral vision.

Secure your glasses. Drill a very small hole through each earpiece, and then pass a nearly invisible fishline "leader" through both earpieces. Tie the leader so short that you can barely squeeze the glasses over your head. Then, even if you make a violent movement, the glasses will not wander very far out of place on your nose.

The worst snow condition, as far as vision is concerned, occurs when flakes of wet snow settle on the lenses. The best solution for this is to wear a Bausch & Lomb Sun Shield over the regular glasses. The shield can be pushed up when too much snow gets on it, and you can then continue until the glasses underneath also become covered with snow. This combination gives you twice as long a run before you have to stop and wipe off the shield and glasses.

Yellow glasses are best for gray days and fog.

There's a new indoor-outdoor sunglass type, Corning's Photogray, which you can get from your optician. For days of mild sun, they work well. When you go out, the action of the sun darkens the glasses, and when you go indoors, the glasses lighten up so that you don't need to remove them. They also make a yellow glass.

Don't buy cheap sunglasses; don't ski with non-plastic prescription glasses; don't ski with glasses unless they are tied to a thread looped around your head, and don't use goggles unless you ski so fast that you need them, because they are hard to wipe off and because they cut down on your peripheral vision.

Chapter 14

SAFETY AND ETIQUETTE

Manners and minding your skiing make a better show

Ski injuries are of a non-permanent kind, ninety-nine times out of a hundred. Fractures, sprains, and dislocations are the most typical ski injuries. There are other occupations such as driving and swimming, where the risk of really permanent injury is much greater. But safety and etiquette are important in skiing, nevertheless.

It is immoral to ski unsafely and to ski impolitely. These two ideas shade into each other. The unmannerly skier is also likely to be the immoral skier, the one who skis out of control.

The first concern of the skier should be for the skiers below him. Whether they are skiing or stationary, he has a duty to keep from running into them.

The rule makes sense. A skier should be able to start onto the trail with the expectation that the skiers coming down the trail will avoid him. Otherwise, the skiers on every trail would have to wait until the last skier on the trail above had stopped before he could take off. This would cause a dangerous jam on every trail.

Therefore, it is the skier coming down the hill who has the duty of avoiding skiers in front of him.

As a matter of keeping the trails clear, assume that the skiers above you will keep clear of you. Don't stand around and wait for every skier on the trail above to come to a standstill. You will jam the trail.

Unfortunately, skiers who are standing tend to be timid about taking off, not realizing that they have the right of way according to the rules of the National Ski Areas Association.

On the other hand, there are too many skiers who don't take seriously the duty of staying clear of skiers below. They feel that they have the right to whiz by and yell "Track!" They don't have that right. As a matter of ski patrol policy, I would like to see the ski patrol lift the ticket of every skier who skis so as to endanger skiers below him. In a season or so, we'd see a definite improvement in trail safety, not to mention manners.

There is a companion rule: the skiers who *are* standing still should stand off to the sides of the trail.

Even if the skier is standing in the middle of the trail, however, the oncoming skier has the duty of steering around him. Again, this makes sense, because the skier standing in the middle of the trail may have come out of his release bindings or may be in some other kind of trouble.

SKI UNDER CONTROL

This rule applies particularly to blind corners. No skier has the right to come around a blind corner or over a blind drop-off so fast that he can't avoid someone standing in the trail. Otherwise, any injured skier would be at the mercy of skiers behind him. If you ski out of control, you might be the skier who runs into an injured skier. Think about that a bit.

One of the first rules of the National Ski Areas Association is that the skier should ski under control. Skiing under control is skiing with the ability to avoid skiers below.

There is a good little trick used by smart skiers to pass by another skier on a narrow trail without disturbing him. (I find that saying "track" or "on your right" or "on your left" is fine, but only when you are just at the moment of passing. Hollering it from way up the hill is likely to confuse the skier below.) The best way to pass is to get into the track of the skier below, make one or two turns exactly where he does, and then, when he makes the next turn, keep going straight. In this way, the skier gets himself out of the way, and whichever way he turns, you clear him.

When you are on a collision course with another skier, pull up. Theoretically, the skier on your left should give way, but you should take the burden of avoiding collision yourself. Don't risk running another skier down just to assert your rights.

Never go launching yourself into the path of an oncoming skier when he is going to have difficulty stopping. That is common sense.

Don't take your skis off and walk on a trail, unless you cannot ski it. The correct way to climb a trail or descend is on your skis. Otherwise, you leave little foot holes that can trip up other skiers.

"Pack out your own bathtub." A bathtub is a big body hole made in soft snow by the fall of a skier. You aren't expected to fill the hole completely, but you should side-step a couple of times up and down over the hole so that you smooth off its edges and it becomes a smooth dip rather than a ragged hole.

A most elementary safety rule is to wear a safety strap on your skis. If the skis release, it is up to you to keep the skis with you. A flying ski, running down the hill on its own, is a nasty projectile.

If you see a ski running loose, be sure to set up the cry, "Ski! Ski!" It will alert everyone

down the hill to a loose ski coming down, so they can get out of its way.

Unless it is moving *very slowly*, don't try to trap anyone's loose ski for him: this is a very dangerous thing to do. The point or edges of a ski, even if it is traveling fairly slowly, will do all kinds of damage to an ankle or shin bone. In the case of a lost ski, you can afford to be callous: the skier who lost the ski is in the wrong. Ninety-nine times out of a hundred, a loose ski simply sails off the trail harmlessly.

COMING TO A STOP

One firm rule, often ignored, is the duty to come to a stop *below* a standing skier. If you come to a stop just above him, you may skid into him. You should not put yourself in the position of endangering another. It isn't part of the sport to scare other skiers.

The exception to this rule is the lift line: you usually have to stop above the lift line, since you can't go below it. Stop and walk *up* to the lift line. Don't come to a stop right *at* it. You may catch an edge and fall into the lift line. This rule is probably the most widely ignored rule in skiing. Every day you will find skiers skiing into skiers in a lift line. I am amazed at the good humor that usually prevails on occasions like this, because it is an avoidable offense.

One of the best ways to keep skiing well is to take plenty of rest stops. Most of all, take a good hour for lunch. This is particularly true on the first day of a weekend or a ski week, when you may be full of energy to begin with and yet become more tired than you realize. A tired skier does not ski well.

In this connection, avoid taking "one last run." It is a superstition among skiers never to say, "Let's take a last run" (it may become your *last* run for a while). The superstition has a good basis in fact. If you are tired and yet tempted to take just one more run, you are stretching it, and this is when you get hurt.

On a cold morning, if you warm up a bit

before you make your first turn, you will have a better first run. The first run, traditionally, is a bad one. The reason is that the skier's muscles and his sense of timing haven't warmed up yet. The quickest way to warm up is to climb up the trail about twenty feet, side-stepping or herringboning, fast. This will get your body ready for the run. It also starts you breathing. One of the big faults of skiers is that they stop breathing quickly when the skiing gets tough. Lack of oxygen in itself is a mental and physical depressant; if you've had a scare, or are skiing badly, stop and take about six good breaths.

These suggestions make the sport sound a bit grim, but it is the overcoming of the "scare" and the transforming of such feelings into a sense of satisfaction at a good run that make skiing a completely captivating sport.

THE SKI PATROL

Most injuries are self-induced, caused by the injured skier himself. In spite of the impoliteness and even foolhardiness of a small percentage of skiers, the excesses of such skiers mostly hurt themselves in the long run.

The ski patrol is a remarkable outfit, composed partly of amateur ski patrolmen who volunteer their time and partly of paid patrolmen who spend all winter at a ski area. (Any given area may have all of one kind or another or a mixture.)

Ski partolmen are trained to give first aid on the slope to injured skiers and to get them down to the bottom, where they can be treated further. Most patrolmen are attached to a specific area. There is a National Patrol, whose members in rust-red parkas are eligible to patrol any ski area. (Membership in the National Patrol is an honor conferred for outstanding service in a local patrol.) The trickiest duty of a patrolman is to get an injured skier onto a toboggan and ski down, holding the toboggan handles (sometimes there is a second patrolman behind) while he guides the toboggan to the bottom.

The first thing to do if a skier is hurt is to summon the patrol. If you are observant, you will have spotted the location of the patrol phones on the various trails. Most of the little shacks at the top of the ski lifts have phones that connect to the patrol. All patrols have a "patrol shack" at the bottom of the area, usually a room in the base building, and there is usually a patrolman there, ready to go.

This brings up a point of safety. The skier should have an area map with him when he goes up the lift. When he goes down a trail, he should know what trail he is on, and approximately how far down the trail he is. This precaution makes skiing more fun (what fun is there in skiing a whole succession of trails when you don't know where you have been?) and it can be extremely helpful in an accident. You can tell the patrol just where the accident is.

For another thing, it will keep you off trails that are either too hard for you or too much of a hike from the lift. (Some trails end as much as a half mile or a mile from any lift). It will keep you from getting lost, and this *can* happen. A friend of mine spent several hours after dark trying to get out of the woods near New York City because he'd gone off on a dead-end trail.

Most ski-area maps, unfortunately, are poor ones. Ski areas won't spend enough money to make accurate, legible maps. And they refuse to mark the trails adequately. Every trail intersection ought to be marked, but it isn't.

Most trail maps do show where the expert trails are, where the intermediate trails are, and so on. And trails have signs at the top, indicating whether the trail is Easy, Difficult, or Most Difficult.

INJURED SKIERS

If a skier is injured, the first skier on the scene should attempt to stay with him and send the next skier down for help, even if it means waiting a bit. The injured skier may become cold and need whatever clothes can be spared him.

segment

The cardinal rule is "Don't move the injured skier." Assume that something is fractured. Leave the skier's boots on. If an ankle is fractured, the boot will act as a cast. (Ankle sprain and fractures are the most common injuries.) Unshackle the ski from his boots, as he lies, but don't pull the boot into a different position. If something is twisted, leave it twisted unless the skier himself (free of the ski) can arrange his position differently. Try to keep the skier warm and quiet, and reassure him that help is on the way. They psychological benefit of having someone to talk to is important.

Once you start moving the skier around, you are taking a risk. Only a trained patrolman can decide properly if it is worth taking or not.

You can increase the damage considerably if you don't know what you are doing.

Again, to alleviate the grim effect of all this, I must point out that the risk of injury is small if the skier knows something about ski technique and stays within terrain that can be handled by this technique. An outstanding example of *not* doing this would be a stem skier going down expert slopes. The stem turn in the hands of a beginning skier simply cannot be shortened enough to make it a safe turn on expert slopes.

If the skier tries to work on his technique and knows what it will do, and if he maintains proper release bindings, he won't have much more chance of injury than he would walking down the sidewalk in a small town.

Chapter   15

COMPETITIVE SKIING, TOURING, AND ACROBATICS

Forms and impact of the alpine racer; the Nordic forms of the sport; flips and fancy skiing

Ski racing is on television these days. We may be coming to a situation where the non-skiing public knows more about the competitive side of the sport than the skiers do. The active skier is likely to be on the slopes on Saturday and Sunday when the ski programs are broadcast. The average skier's reaction to a race is that a trail will be closed for public use, more's the pity.

Things may be changing a bit. The impact of television on the alpine races (slalom, giant slalom, downhill) has made the race committees conscious of the public relations necessary to interest spectators. Televised races now start on time and proceed briskly. Public-address systems inform the spectators of the time and standing of each racer. Occasionally we see an American race with some four thousand people lining the course and staying until the race is over. We are a long way from the European situation, where crowds of ten and twenty thousand are normal, but the interest in racing is growing, even among the skiers. Denver has won the right to hold the 1976 Winter Olympics, and that will boost national interest. In addition, ex-national coach Bob Beattie has established a pro league.

The three forms of competition closest to the downhill recreational form are the three alpine races—the slalom, giant slalom, and downhill. Slalom is a race set through gates made up of paired slalom poles. The poles are set loosely in the snow, so that if a racer strikes one, he'll knock it aside. The racer's ski must pass to the inside of the pole, even if he knocks it over. Otherwise he is disqualified. He must also pass through every gate, although he has a choice of entering from either side.

SLALOM GATES

Gates fall into two types: the *closed gate*, in which both poles of the gate are set in the fall line, one below the other, and the *open gate*, in which the poles are set across the fall line from each other, side by side on the hill. Two closed gates in a row constitute a "hairpin" and three or more constitute a "flush."

One can almost say that wedel was invented in the flush. To negotiate a flush successfully and quickly, the ski racer must make the short, connected, reverse-powered turns that we call wedel. (Germans use this word in two forms:

280. *Slalom. Guy Perillat, one of the greatest racers in history, going through a slalom gate at Stowe: reverse shoulder and angulation show how the recreational style and racing style have the comma in common.*

wedel, the verb; *Wedeln,* the noun.) Properly, it is "wedel turn" and "Austrian wedeln." But the latter trips the American tongue and most of us say "wedel" for both noun and adjective. The word "wedel" is well on the way to becoming a single-form expression in our language, whether verb, noun, or adjective.

Getting back to racing, the point has been made that the wedel was invented by racers. This is true of all of our advanced skiing forms. Yesterday's advanced recreational skiing form is today's intermediate form, and what was intermediate yesterday is a beginner turn today. The wedel turn started out as a racing turn, became the trademark of the expert recreational skier, and is now being performed by newcomers to the sport in GLM schools.

If only because some racing forms eventually come down to the recreational skier, all skiers are in debt to racing. *Avalement,* developed by

racers to accelerate in a turn, is a sit-back turn which is great over a bump. Today you see good skiers everywhere using it in moguls.

The other part of racing's gift to skiing is that the racing side of the sport gives skiing the kind of publicity needed to make the sport grow. The sport should continue to grow in numbers. The only way that skiing can survive as a healthy sport is to keep on growing. Some of the conservative members of the sport have bemoaned the impact of the mass skier, but as they complain they are very likely going down a run that never would have existed but for the "mass skier," off a lift that was built, not because skiing is a grand old sport, but because skiing is expanding.

The second form of alpine racing is the giant slalom. Whereas the gates in slalom are usually close-set, with sixty or eighty gates in the course, giant slalom gates are set further apart. The turns, rather than being short and sharp, are long and smooth. Slalom is more like skiing a mogul hill in the East, while giant slalom is more like skiing in the wide-open terrain of the West.

In either the slalom or giant slalom form, the skier usually "comes in high" on the gates. That is, he tries to skin just the inside or the uphill pole of a gate. This gives him a better position when he comes out to attack the next gate. Once you are low on one gate, it is hard to make the next gate. The skier on a giant slalom course more often has a choice of high or low, since he has more time to pick his course and needs less margin for error.

There is a specific racing turn that is not yet incorporated into recreational skiing systems, except as an exercise. This turn is a "skating turn." It often makes for a faster route between gates. In the skating turn, the skier simply "goes with" the inside ski as he comes out of the fall line to finish a turn. He puts his weight on it by means of a skating motion. He pushes himself onto that uphill ski. Once the skier is riding the uphill ski entirely, he brings the downhill ski up parallel. Riding the inside ski allows the skier to lunge forward onto

281. *Billy Kidd, recent world champion, finishing a long, sweeping turn into a giant slalom gate. Turns are longer, speeds higher than in slalom.*

it as he comes out of his turn, so that he is ahead of his skis rather than behind them. Also, it allows him to get a "higher line" to the next gate.

The secret of the good slalom and giant slalom racer is his ability to predict his path. The best turn between gates is that turn that uses just enough edging all the way through to carve into the gate at the maximum desirable spot. If the skier over-edges early in the turn, he will have to flatten the skis later in the turn to lengthen it out.

A very expert slalom skier usually under-edges in the turn and jams his edges a bit to make it through the gate. This gives him a straighter, faster path. In giant slalom, the perfect turn has even edging all the way. This calls for exquisite edge control.

Much has been made of the improved start that international racers have been practicing. They back up and come lunging through the gate, thrusting themselves forward by the arms so that they hit the starting gate at eight or ten miles an hour instead of starting from a dead standstill. Jean-Claude Killy has been outstand-

ing in his accomplishment of the running start; he attributes a good deal of his success in winning the first two World Cups as well as his triple Olympic win in 1968 to his fast starts.

THE DOWNHILL RACE

The downhill, the third form of alpine racing, is a thing unto itself. With a few exceptions, the great slalom and giant slalom racers have been only medium-good downhillers, while some of the best downhill racers do not figure in slalom and giant slalom betting. The younger racers, typically, are best at downhill, make their name there, and then go on to become good slalom runners after losing their touch in downhill.

The great development in the art of downhill racing came around 1960, when the French made great strides in this event, inventing an aerodynamically sound squatting position, which they dubbed *l'oeuf*, or "the egg," so-called because it looked like an egg when seen from the side.

282. *Leo Lacroix, starting into a skating turn during a downhill run. He will put his weight on the inside ski at this point, letting the outside ski drop away.*

The downhill course is essentially a trail that has been cleared of most of the moguls and designed for speeds of fifty to seventy miles an hour. A winner often averages better than sixty. The racers try to stay low, in the egg or similar posture, to reduce wind resistance. They "prejump" the bumps to keep their skis on the snow, since they have less air resistance that way. Jumping into the air is spectacular but slow.

With the exception of Bill Beck and Buddy Werner back in the last decade, the United States has not had any startling successes in downhill. This seems to be the one event that is the province of the French and Austrians, with an occasional outside European, such as Switzerland's Roger Staub, coming on as a threat.

In general the recent trend of the United States abroad has been toward better performance as a team, partly as a result of the more comprehensive national training programs initiated by Bob Beattie (now retired) when he became the first full-time coach that the United States had ever had.

In the 1964 Olympics, the Americans took the first two medals ever taken by American men in Olympic or world championship competition. (The world championship, or FIS [International Ski Federation], as it is called, takes place every two years, and when there are Olympic games, the same races serve as both world and Olympic championships.) The Americans were Billy Kidd, second in slalom, and Jim Huega, third. Jean Saubert continued the fairly good record that American women have had in medal-winning by coming in third in the slalom.

In the 1968 Olympics, however, the United States won no medals. In the 1970 World Cup championships, Billy Kidd *won* the combined, to give the United States its first world champion.

The future of the American team will in all likelihood depend on the success of the new coach in getting nationwide quality racing programs going in the United States; ten or fifteen

283. *The late Bud Werner. For a long time Bud was the only consistent United States threat to the European aces.*

such continuous programs at a minimum, so that a fairly broad base for future teams can be established.

Our system now includes full-time coaches, races in season in Europe and with European racers in the United States during annual World Cup competitions (started in 1967). The training program for United States racers starts with conditioning training in the fall. The program is designed to bring the national coach and all the best talent in the United States together.

Some old-timers may yearn for the days when American skiers abroad were a rare and sometimes beautiful thing: Bud Werner winning the Holmenkollen downhill (the first American to win a European race), Andy Mead Lawrence coming back with a fistful of medals from Cortina at eighteen—then things were really amateur. But, for better or worse, the United States has entered the international race scene on a firm and continuing basis, and the results should eventually show it even more strongly than now.

Bud Werner deserves special mention. He was the first American to show the Europeans that an American could win anything, any time. He was not consistent, just consistently dangerous. He was killed in an avalanche when he retired from racing, after the 1964 Olympics. But he had proved that you can come out of the United States and compete on the same level as the Austrians and French. They worried about him whenever he showed up at the starting line.

NORDIC EVENTS

This brings us to the other half of the competitive sport, the Nordic events: jumping and cross-country, plus a combination of cross-country and target-shoot called biathlon.

Jumping doesn't have much in common with alpine skiing except that the skis are roughly, only roughly, similar. The jumping ski is a longer, broader job with more grooves on the bottom and no steel edges on the corners.

The art of ski jumping consists of making a dive off the platform, or inrun, of the jump. As long as the skier holds a good forward position in the air, he doesn't have to move very much. Then he must gracefully accept the shock of landing, some thirty to one hundred yards down the hill, and stand up through the outrun, so that he collects maximum points.

Historically, the alpine and jumping events —and cross-country, too, for that matter—grew up together, often being combined in one race. There were races in which you climbed to the top of the hill, ran down in a beeline, took off over a jump, dodged some trees in a kind of natural slalom, and came out at the end as an all-around racer, if you finished at all. These events were called by various names: "kneikalom," "hopalom," and "slalom," with only the last-named surviving into modern times as a name.

Twenty years ago, skiers were more all-around performers. It was long considered the best kind of win if you could win a four-way meet: the original "ski-meister" concept was that you were the best if you had top total for jumping, cross-country, slalom, and downhill. Today, the specialists have taken over, and praises go to the individual-event champs. The one exception is the "Nordic combined," a jump and cross-country taken together, whose winner is a pale survivor of the stalwarts who could do everything.

Jumping today is a measure of the specializing that has taken place. Good jumpers go off the jump hundreds of times in a year's training; years back, fifty or so jumps might have been tops for the season. But the jumper today goes farther; the early records talk about twenty yards, and today we talk about one hundred yards (about ninety meters); on a few very large hills known as "ski-flying hills" (not used for Olympic events), there are skiers who have gone over two hundred meters.

A hill is designed for a certain average length of jump, say ninety meters. The slope of the hill closely follows the line of the skier's trajectory so that the landing is not too violent. When he jumps the larger hills, his take-off speed is one factor that determines how far the jumper will go. The other is how the jumper "rides the air." He must keep his arms close in to the sides or dead ahead of him, so as to have minimum air resistance and, at the same time, he must bend forward so that his back is all but horizontal to the skis. This makes the jumper's back into a kind of airfoil and gives him a "lift" down the hill. Half the points scored are for the distance and half are for form. Form depends on how closely the skier approximates the ideal airfoil and how quietly he holds that form.

Jumping is a top Scandinavian spectator sport and is a good draw in the Midwest, where there

284. *Jumping. Ansten Samuelstuen exhibiting good form. His forward lean is giving him a good airfoil shape. He would be marked down slightly for the fact that his skis are not exactly parallel. Samuelstuen held the North American jump record for several years.*

are lots of spectators of Scandinavian descent. The United States has never taken a world medal in jumping but did take a first in the combined jump at the 1968 Holmenkollen.

CROSS-COUNTRY

The American record in cross-country is poor. Typical American finalists run well back in the longer European cross-country world-class championships. The reason seems to be a lack of realization on the part of our coaches that Scandinavia can show them something when it comes to training and technique.

The main cross-country events are 15 kilometers, 30 kilometers, 50 kilometers, and the 5-kilometer dash. One United States mile is about 1.6 kilometers, and so these races are about 10 miles, 20 miles, 30 miles, and 3 miles, roughly.

The cross-country skier is the peerless athlete

285. *Cross-country. The skier has just kicked off from the left ski and is gliding forward on the right ski. Next, he'll kick off from the gliding ski and the other ski will glide ahead.*

in the eyes of the northern countries of Europe —Russia, Norway, Finland, Sweden, and Denmark. Any man among them would rather come in the drained victor in a thirty-mile, three-hour marathon than be the hero of sixty seconds of fast action on a slalom course.

There is no doubt that the kind of skier who can come up to snuff in the cross-country events has virtues that are rare and uncommonly pleasant. There are no "hot-shot" cross-country runners. They are wiry and usually soft-spoken.

Cross-country skiers use skis that are narrow and small by comparison with the alpine. The whole outfit—boots, skis, bindings, and poles—weighs less than a pair of alpine *boots;* this makes it easier for the cross-country racer to keep up his speed.

The art of waxing cross-country skis is a necessary skill. The wax must be of such a consistency that it will "grab" the snow when the skier's weight is on the ski, and slide well across the snow when the skier shoves it forward. This may seem impossible, but, because of the structure of snow, it can be done. The wax engages the separate flakes of snow under stationary pressure, but slides over them once the ski has started sliding.

The technique of cross-country racing is in "kicking off" from one ski, sliding the other ahead, getting the weight on that, then kicking off onto the next. It is a series of kickoffs and glides, producing a steady, relatively effortless speed of ten or twelve miles an hour over the flat—about the equivalent of a five-minute mile—for distances of ten miles or more. Going uphill, the cross-country skiers rely on good wax and their arms. They go straight up. Going downhill (there are some pretty steep downhills in a cross-country race, at times), they rely on good balance plus step-turns and skating turns. Cross-country skis have no edges to speak of, and they don't make parallel turns readily.

SKI TOURING

The "civilian" form of cross-country is called "touring." Ski touring is an obsessive sport in Norway. The same is true, to a lesser degree, in Sweden. Britons, Russians, Finns (almost as rabid as Norwegians), and the Alpine countries (in the form of high-mountain touring) all go in quite heavily for touring on cross-country skis. The United States and Japan lag in touring. This is too bad, because touring can be one of the pleasantest occupations a skier can have, equal in quality to an occasional rare run in fine powder snow. In touring, you move at a comfortable pace, set to the slowest in the group. You can be continuously companionable as you walk, and you are outdoors in the quiet, away from machinery and crowds and man-made paths. Lots of touring is done over unbroken snow, away from any distraction but nature. There isn't anything more genuinely appreciated by a skier than this kind of atmosphere, if he is a bone-deep skier.

What enables touring to be so popular in Norway and other northern countries is the existence of touring trails for day touring, and of longer trails set with huts or hotels for overnight and week-long touring in the mountains. A skier who can come in at the end of a great day's walk to a nicely lit fire and a good hearty buffet is not going to miss the elbow-bending jostle of an after-ski weekend at a lift area.

SKI ACROBATICS

A whole new phase of the sport has been initiated by the movies, particularly the work of a group of inspired film-makers at Summit Films in Denver. The film-makers who started Summit, Barry Corbet and Roger Brown, turned out a series of inspired films using skiers who could Charleston, do flips (as many as three somersaults in one jump) and unbelievable jumps and drops. The star of the films was an American, Tom Leroy, who could do more fantastic things than any of his fellow skiing stunt men. You can see him by getting (from Hart Ski) the latest Summit creations, *The Outer Limits, Moebius Flip,* and *The Great Ski Chase.*

Chapter 16

WHERE TO SKI

A rundown on the United States and Canada

Major resorts in the United States divide into several different regions. (A major resort is one that has a number of big lifts, a nearby ski village with plenty of lodging, and after-ski entertainment.) The most populous ski country is in the East, where two thirds of the skiers live. The East's great playground is New England, and next comes the state of New York. There are ski areas farther south: Pennsylvania, New Jersey, and down the "banana belt" of skiing, the Smokies and Blue Ridge portion of the southern Appalachian chain.

- The foremost ski resort in the East is Stowe, Vermont. Stowe has been tops in the business longer than any area in the East, and it still holds the number-one prestige position. The expert runs of the area, taken as a whole, are the steepest and most challenging terrain in the East. The skier who negotiates Nose Dive, Lift Line, the National, the Goat, and the Starr, has really put away some skiing. Stowe also has intermediate and beginner sections: the Lord trail leads to a T-bar that supports a complex of easier trails, and there is a separate area, Spruce Peak, with two chairs built for the beginner and the intermediate. In their gondola lift runs, they have excellent advanced intermediate runs.

North of Stowe, there is only one large area: Jay Peak, situated near the Canadian border. It has a large new cable-car lift and a maze of good trails.

South of Stowe in Vermont, there is a threesome: Glen Ellen, Sugarbush, and Mad River Glen, all within a few miles of each other. The

287. *Typical eastern trail skiing at Killington, Vermont.*

combined lifts and runs of the three make this region competitive with Stowe. There are lots of after-ski places and lots of lodges, and it is an hour nearer the big cities. Sugarbush has a name for glamour. Mad River's top trails are as excit-ing as Stowe's. Glen Ellen is an extremely good intermediate mountain. West of this again is Bolton Valley, a big area that has specialized in beginner terrain.

South of this is the mid-Vermont complex: Killington, Pico Peak, and Okemo. The latter two are smaller: good places to get well away from the crowds. Killington has three separate but connected areas and is set in a valley full of inns and with a good after-ski place, the Wobbly Barn, famous for its rock and roll. The new Kill-ington gondola opens five miles of runs under it; it is the wonder of mid-Vermont.

SOUTHERN VERMONT

The southern Vermont complex consists of Bromley, Magic Mountain, Stratton, Mount Snow, and Haystack, plus a sprinkling of smaller areas that don't quite come up to major status. Mount Snow is a supermarket of skiing, with more trails and more lifts than any other area in the East. Stratton has a beautiful base lodge, fewer trails, and a name for sophistication. Bromley is almost as venerable as Stowe, and it has lovely intermediate trails and a very good snow-making set-up, which often saves the skiing for its customers. Haystack, the newest and smallest, is a mountain that is set in chalets, as an over-all development of living-skiing. Magic has some good expert trails and is much less crowded than any of the others.

THE NEW YORK AREA

In New York, the giant in the north is White-face, near Lake Placid, constantly expanding, with the longest and highest runs in the East. In north and west New York there are a number of very good small areas. Snow Ridge at Turin, is the best-known. South, along the New York Thruway, going up from New York City, are the Catskill areas: Belleayre is the largest, with an excellent beginner area and some good ex-pert pitches; Hunter Mountain is far the largest in size and in accommodations round about. The Catskills, largely, are intermediate terrain, but they are near enough to New York City to make it possible to drive up for the day.

Brody and Jiminy Peak, in the northwest corner of Massachusetts, are within reach of New Yorkers for day skiing, and are the largest areas in that state. In Pennsylvania, Camelback is the queen area, with good intermediate trails and a fine base lodge. New Jersey's top area is Great Gorge, fifty miles from Times Square.

NEW HAMPSHIRE AND MAINE

Cannon Mountain is the physical giant in New Hampshire. It has a cable car, lots of T-bar lifts, and some wonderful trails. There are a good many places to stay round about. After-ski drinking places are not so plentiful as in Ver-mont, but the skiers tend to be more serious

288. One of the two base complex buildings at Mount Tecumseh in Waterville Valley, New Hamp-shire. This building contains a cafeteria, nursery, and post office. The other building, not shown, houses medical dispensary, ski shop with Head rent-als and repairs, as well as the administrative office.

289. *Mount Snow is a modern, open-slope-and-trail layout, with miles and miles of ski running available on the Vermont mountain.*

anyway. The nearest area to Cannon of any size is Waterville Valley, designed for intermediates; it draws more skiers than Cannon; it is run by ex-Olympian Tom Corcoran. In the next valley

291. *Belleayre, New York, summit overlooks typical Catskill scenery. The area is within a few hours' drive of New York City.*

east we have Wildcat, facing Mount Washington. Wildcat's gondola-car lift keeps you out of the wind. A bit south is Cranmore, with its Skimobile, the first major lift in the East, and other lifts besides. Cranmore is in North Conway, a lively ski town.

South in New Hampshire, the big areas are Mount Sunapee, Mount Whittier (gondola-car lift), and Gunstock, with its ski school run by Penny Pitou, our number-one woman Olympic racer in 1960.

In Maine, farthest East, there is only one

290. *Rugged Presidential Range rings the ski area at Cannon Mountain, New Hampshire.*

292. *The only above-timberline lift skiing in the East is to be had off the gondola lift at Sugarloaf, Maine.*

really big area, Sugarloaf. It has a gondola lift and miles of trails. There are a number of smaller, very pleasant ski areas north and south in the state.

WEST OF THE APPALACHIANS

From the west side of the Appalachians to the east side of the Rockies, there is a long stretch of north country with lots of small hills and small ski areas. There are a few good middle-sized areas as well, but nothing to excite the expert skier. The best-known of the midwest resorts is Boyne Mountain, Michigan. Boyne has

a modest elevation, but lots of expensive lodging and chic people. It also has ex-Olympian Othmar Schneider as ski-school head. There's a new area, Lake Geneva Playboy Club in Wisconsin, with a stunning hotel and real Playboy bunnies.

THE ROCKIES

The Rockies are the real goal of avid skiers in the United States. The fabled Aspen, Colorado, has three great mountains, full of steeps, pitches, and variations. The town of Aspen has the finest display of after-ski that the country affords. It is the skier's City of Lights. There are four ski areas at Aspen: the beginner-intermediate Buttermilk; the new development at Snowmass, which is wooded, glade-type country, with intermediate grades; and Aspen Highlands, with expert terrain, besides the main, renowned mountain, Ajax. Ajax's trails—Ruthie's Run, Copper Bowl, Gentleman's Ridge, Spar Gulch—are hard to duplicate.

Vail is newer and swankier and quieter. It has a smaller village and the mountain is great, but slightly less expert than Aspen's. Vail is built on rolling hills. Vail also has a couple of unique bowls that provide superb powder skiing on the far side of its development.

A huge area is going in just west of the continental divide: Keystone; worth watching.

Arapahoe Basin is the highest Colorado area, at thirteen thousand feet; it has spring skiing way into May and very often glorious spring weather.

Winter Park, Loveland, and Berthoud Pass share the ridge of the Continental Divide with Arapahoe. The four are within an easy drive of Denver, which makes Denver a fabulous town for those who *have* to work and *like* to ski.

Breckenridge, next to Vail, is a smaller area with people who like the small-town atmosphere. Breckenridge is almost a museum piece in its entirety, preserving some of the architecture and atmosphere of the Old West. Mount Werner, farthest west in the state of Colorado, is named for Bud Werner, who was born and who learned to race in the nearby resort of Steamboat Springs. It is working toward status as a first-rate ski area, but at present is quite modest. Denver, site of the 1976 Winter Olympics, is building at least one new resort in the foothills of the Rockies.

Southernmost in the Rockies are the "southwest areas," Red River, Taos, Santa Fe, Sandia Peak, and Sierra Blanca, all in New Mexico. These draw a good many Texas skiers. Taos is big stuff, with great runs, and snow is never a problem. The others are smaller. Sierra Blanca is a lone white tower and the closest to Texas; consequently, it has been all "Tex-ified." Both Sandia (which is right inside the city limits of Albuquerque) and Sierra Blanca have cable-car lifts.

But, for the ultimate in powder, the skier will usually do somewhat better in the Wasatch Range outside Salt Lake City. This is the best powder in the ski world—Europe or the United States. The reason is that the weather is dry. (Moisture in the air makes powder snow into non-powder.) The areas clustered outside Salt Lake—Alta, Brighton, Solitude, Treasure, Snow Park, and Timp Haven—have deep, dry snow. The top resort is Alta. The runs here are more extensive and more expert. Alta has just begun to develop its potential terrain, as well, even though it has been in the business a long time. Snowbird, a new resort, just south of Alta, is making a good start at being Alta's competition.

Just north of all of this is Wyoming, with one vast area being built and expanding yearly: Jackson Hole. This is in the Tetons, and has the most spectacular scenery in the United States. Jackson will be the biggest area in the country when it is finished. It has the biggest total drop and the longest trails.

The other "name" area in the Rockies is Sun Valley. It is the oldest of the western areas, having been founded at one glittering swoop by Union Pacific, and has maintained its prestige as the most exclusive resort in the nation. It is set in the middle of the southern part of Idaho and has its own "village" distinct from the nearby town of Ketchum. There are swank rates and moderate rates in Sun Valley. The Janss brothers, resort specialists and developers of Snowmass, have recently taken over Sun Valley; its lift system is being expanded and an extensive home-building development is being planned. Sun Valley's famous Exhibition Trail, its great powder bowls, its wonderful Warm Springs run, are enough reason to consider this and Aspen as the Big Two in the West.

North of Sun Valley again, on the Canadian border, we have Big Mountain in Montana, noted for the great steep run down its main face and its late snow. Big Mountain ranks with Arapahoe as a spring ski resort. A huge new re-

293. *Sun Valley's Mount Baldy lies high over the town of Ketchum (extreme right), just down the road from the village of Sun Valley. The area has a name as the most plush in the United States.*

sort, Big Sky, headed by Chet Huntley of television newscasting fame, is being readied in the center of the state.

THE COAST

To get the only year-round skiing in the United States, you would have to go to the West Coast, over to Mount Baker, Washington. (The snow gets a bit dirty in late July, but there's new snow a-comin'.) Seattle is ringed by a series of big and very busy ski areas: Stevens Pass, Crystal Mountain, White Pass, Alpenthal, and Snoqualmie. The ski-school operations tend to be very large here, and there are more people learn-ing to ski per square mile of snow around Seattle than anywhere in the country. As a ski city, Seattle ranks with Denver.

A bit farther south, in Oregon, is a second volcanic cone (Mount Baker is a volcanic peak), Mount Hood. Like Baker, it rears into the air far above its neighbors. Mount Hood is the site of a summer racing camp, and it, too, can run year around if the skiers come. The showpiece of Mount Hood is the Timberline Lodge, a great, ornate, grandiose structure built during the 1930s when the government was sponsoring projects for local artisans and artists. The lodge is worth a trip up the mountain, even if you don't ski. Hoodoo Ski Bowl is the other Oregon ski area of note, having two chairs to Mount Hood's five.

294. *Junior Bounous skiing the powder on Sugar Bowl's Mount Lincoln.*

295. *The Lodge, Mammoth Inn, at Mammoth Mountain, California.*

In northern California, there are two rather remote resorts with good skiing: at Lassen Peak and Mount Shasta. Shasta has one of the most formidable-looking ski bowls in the world and lots of open terrain. Lassen has volcanic steam pits at the bottom of its runs and beautiful scenery.

In central California, we have a cluster of resorts on the Nevada-California border, directly east from San Francisco, an easy drive. The most famous, of course, is Squaw Valley, where the United States held its second Winter Olympics in 1960. This has become a fantastically large complex of lifts and trails. The valley itself is full of lodges and homes, and up on the mountain one gondola and thirteen chair lifts buzz skiers up. Their latest lift is a big cable car which carries 130 people in one swoop.

The next most renowned in Central California is a smaller, quieter, and most picturesque place: Sugar Bowl. There are no cars in the village, because all skiers come in from an outside parking lot via a "Magic Carpet" lift that goes into the village. The mountain is known for good expert terrain and good dry snow.

The next resort in line, in terms of fame, is Heavenly Valley, on Lake Tahoe, just east of Squaw Valley. Heavenly is at the south end of Tahoe and has a commanding view of it. The area has five chairs and a gondola lift. It is expanding as fast as Squaw.

Bear Valley is a brand-new resort south of Squaw Valley with some of the most magnificent scenery in the state.

South of the mid-state cluster is Mammoth. This is a very high and, during the winter, very dry-snow mountain, competing in quality with Alta. The snow stays to June, too, so that Mammoth has it both ways. Mammoth has five chairs and a gondola going up the great saddle of Mammoth Peak. The lodge at Mammoth is an architectural triumph.

Farthest south in California is a group of smaller resorts serving Los Angeles skiers. The largest is Mount Baldy, the queen of the San Bernadino resorts, with three chairs and twenty-one hundred feet of vertical drop.

CANADA

Canada has resorts too, some of top rank.

Just north of New Hampshire and Vermont there is the Quebec City entry in the big time: Mont Sainte Anne, with a seventy-seven-hundred-foot gondola lift. To the west, north of New York State, is the Montreal cluster: the biggest is Mont Tremblant, with most of the very good expert terrain. About ten smaller resorts are gathered nearby, most of them attached to hotels. The hospitality and the French-Canadian cuisine make the trip north to the Montreal cluster worthwhile, the terrain of Mont Tremblant aside. In western Quebec, above Ottawa, one big resort is Mont Sainte Marie.

In the Canadian Rockies, near Banff, are three areas: Lake Louise, with its great aerial tram, and Mount Norquay with nearby Sunshine. Sunshine is going to have a big development in the near future. What it offers now is snow and marvelous scenery, on a par with that near Jackson Hole.

On the Canadian West Coast there are a number of resorts on the considerable heights outside Vancouver. The largest is Mount Seymour, which looks right down on the city. North a bit is Garibaldi, with one big aerial lift and a few ordinary chairs, but it is a mountain with ambitions of the Olympic sort, having the biggest vertical drops of any developed area on the continent, forty-three hundred feet, just a bit more than Jackson Hole.

This leaves us the banana belt, that surprising swath of resorts in the southern Appalachians for skiers out of Washington, D.C., Baltimore, and other cities. None of them except the Homestead, in Virginia, has attracted much national attention, but it is nice that they are all there and waiting for those out of easy reach of the snowier north country.